Claim Your Space™
Spirit Attachment

Ghost Symptoms
Break the Spell and Be Well

Kelly Kiernan Ray

Names have been changed to protect clients' rights to privacy.

Copyright © 2009 by Kelly Kiernan Ray

All rights reserved, including the right to reproduce this book or portions thereof in any form.

Cover art by Robin Urton www.eyeconart.net

To my family - Carle, Sean and Fiona - for unswerving support through all the years of sessions, and the writing of this book.

To Patty, my beloved friend and teacher, who showed me the doorway out of pain and limitation into healing and Light.

To those who came before me, for everything.

Contents

Preface

Glossary of Terms

1.	My Dilemma	1
2.	The Vortex of Hell	15
3.	How Spirits Get Attached to Us	33
4.	In the Spin and Out Again	51
5.	Healing and Religion	63
6.	Suicide and Spirit Attachment	89
7.	Symptoms	111
8.	Sudden Death and Other Situations	127
9.	You're Not Crazy	141
10.	Case Study – Jeannie	157
11.	Claiming Your Space	177
12.	Keeping your Life Condition Strong	199

Preface

Because this book focuses on trauma and haunting, it seems like all I talked about was the bad stuff in my childhood. It doesn't mean there weren't good times, too. There were many. I feel the need to balance that out, here. I did my best to tell, analytically, a very painful story, in an attempt to help other people who may find themselves in similar circumstances. I drew heavily from my personal life for illustrative purposes, and to show readers how to look for patterning. I zeroed in on the subject matter, which is how trauma sticks in the human energy field, and how to get well.

For the sake of my family it must be said, we had intelligent, well-educated and talented parents. They both served overseas in World War two – my father in the Army Office of Strategic Services, and my mother in the American Red Cross. My mother obtained her Bachelor of Arts degree, learned several languages and became a teacher. She was a skilled tennis player and ballroom dancer. She sang and played the piano, was upbeat, humorous, loving and generous in continuously overwhelming circumstances.

My father had unique gifts and interests. He had a photographic memory, was a Judo expert and gourmet Chinese cook. He learned the language so he could write the recipes in

Mandarin. He was artistic in multiple media, a textile craftsman - designing costumes, weaving, sewing and working with leather - a painter, anatomical artist, musician, astrologer with his own column, and psychic. Though not formally educated like my mother, my father was said to be intelligent and charismatic.

My siblings are and were kind, smart and courageous people. We went to private schools off and on, were taught good manners and social skills, exposed to music, culture and travel. We had adventures and happy times, like hosting dinner parties, skiing in Vermont, touring the inside of the Great Pyramid at Giza in Egypt, going to Niagara Falls, spending winter breaks in the Bahamas. We engaged in civic duties like providing refreshments to local firemen while they battled large (and historic) structure fires, volunteering to care for displaced persons during the Blizzard of 1978, heading up the Unicef drive for the local school district. As spirits choosing a life path, they are/were the bravest of the brave, suffering untold heartbreak in the haunted house, undoubtedly for an unknown higher purpose. My love goes out to all of them.

What amazes me is the patterning I see in everything. Learning to look for patterning was a blessing because it put so many things into perspective. The swirl of events that made up our childhood was so intense it swallowed up some of us, and made it impossible to have perspective at the time. But in order to survive and not be permanently disabled by childhood events, viewing patterning - understanding our place in it and how to change it - is of vital importance.

It may be said I am searching for explanations. Perhaps that is true. But what I learned in the course of my own healing was so profound I feel I would be absolutely remiss not to share it. It is my cherished hope readers will learn valuable insights and skills by reading this book, and delve into their own patterning with the knowledge that they are fully capable of healing themselves and becoming happier and healthier than ever, regardless of what they have been through.

Glossary of Terms

Aura – The body of energy surrounding every living being. See also, human energy field.

Claim Your Space™ –Technique by which people can free themselves of debilitating energy forms. See chapter 11.

Clear – To free someone's aura, ergo physical, mental and emotional bodies, of debilitating energy forms.

Density - The concentration of people or things within an area in relation to its size. Densities in the human energy field, caused by traumatic experience or by spirit attachment, can cause illness.

Energy healing – A form of healing that focuses on the human energy field, eliminating symptoms in the physical body by approaching them at the root.

Ghost - A person's life essence no longer in its physical body. See also *spirit*.

Grace - In Christian and Hindu philosophies, the infinite love, mercy, favor and goodwill shown to humankind by God.

Haunted - Invaded by a foreign energy. Similar to possessed, but usually associated with a place.

Host – an organism which, consciously or unconsciously, provides space for another organism to live.

Glossary of Terms, continued

Human energy field – the aura or subtle bodies of energy surrounding every human being.

Karma - in Hindu and Buddhist philosophies, it means *action* in thought, word and deed. The quality of one's current life is determined by one's behavior in this and in previous lives. Karma is fluid, changeable, based on your actions.

Life Condition – Buddhist term for vibrational frequency. See definition for vibrational frequency below.

Possessed – The condition of a person hosting the life force of another human being. Demonic possession not addressed in this book.

Psychic - able to perceive nonphysical activity or information outside the sphere of scientific knowledge.

Past life trauma - patterning caused by frightening or shattering experiences from a previous lifetime, affecting you in current time, manifesting in fears or other symptoms.

Reiki – Universal Life Force Energy, can be received as a healing experience, or received in the form of an attunement, which enables one to transmit the energy as a healer.

spirit – (lower case) the life essence of a person that is no longer in its own body. See also, *ghost*.

Glossary of Terms, continued

Spirit – (upper case) God, Divinity, Source of All That Is.

Spirit attachment – The condition of having the spirit of a deceased person in one's energy field – possession.

Spirit depossession – The process by which the attached spirit is released from one's human energy field.

Symptoms – manifestations in the physical body of abnormalities in the human energy field. They may manifest emotionally, mentally or physically.

Trauma – Emotional shock caused by an extremely distressing experience that fractures the human psyche, causing imprinting (density) in the human energy field that manifests in the physical as fears, phobias, obsessions, illness, etc.

Vibrational frequency – the speed at which your human energy field vibrates. When one is full of traumatic densities, one's vibrational frequency is said to be "low", affecting the health of the organism. When one prays, meditates or chants, does altruistic deeds or receives energy healing, one's vibrational frequency can be "raised" bringing about an increase in vitality and good health.

Vortex - a whirling mass of energy that draws everything nearby into itself.

My Dilemma

It was my 45th birthday. My 18 year old son berated me mercilessly, saying I was the craziest person he knew, and all I did was sit around talking to people about ghosts on the internet while my husband worked twelve hours a day. Of course, he was exaggerating. Later he said, "Don't listen to me, I'm just a stupid teenager!" But the poison had been injected and I was full of self-doubt.

We had recently moved to a new state after having lived 18 years in the San Francisco Bay Area, California. In six months, I had been unable to find employment in my new domicile. Not that I hadn't tried. My Work folder was full of cover letters, job applications and rejection notices. I was receiving emails daily from job-search websites. I had signed up with several staffing agencies. I had spent hours composing different spins on cover letters, in hopes I would crack the code, and finally say the right thing to afford me an interview. But, nothing. My best friend Patty said "there's a reason you're not finding work… you're *SUPPOSED* to be doing something *ELSE*! You're supposed to be writing this book!"

I was struggling with my identity, I suppose, right on time for a mid life crisis. I was unwilling to leave behind all the skill and experience I had accumulated over a fourteen-year period, working with a psychic, clearing people's past life trauma and doing spirit depossession. I was feeling very wobbly, without my second wheel. Patty French, my cohort in these psychic sessions, had been my best friend for fourteen years, and now we were 800 miles apart. In my mind, she was the talented one, the one to whom we should literally bow down in reverence and awe. Her ability – to, see right into another person's energy bodies and identify not only areas that had sustained trauma, but also the presence of other people's spirits - continuously astounded and enthralled me. Without her I felt inadequate, yet still determined it was my mission to help people who were beset with this sort of problem. After all, I knew from personal experience.

Now that I had made the economically-minded-move-for-the-good-of-the-family, I found myself simply unable to give up all the "spirit stuff." It was profoundly frustrating that my area of expertise was something my more conservative friends referred to as "woo-woo," so weird you can't just blurt it out at cocktail parties or PTA meetings.

"And what do you do, Kelly?"

"Well…"

It's not that we ever made a living at it. In fact, there always seemed to be something of a religious/spiritual taboo about charging money to free people of possessing spirits. Yet I still felt this was my calling, my reason for being, and we spent countless hours having individual and group sessions, teaching classes and offering counseling.

ಙ

I seem to know when persons are afflicted with an attached spirit. They seem to be dropped in my lap. It became quite funny to my psychic partner. If someone in my vicinity, either in person or on the internet, is having a problem with spirits, somehow it is brought to my attention, and I am able to get right to the heart of the matter, giving them instructions on how to claim their space and strengthen their vibrational frequency to avoid further invasion. For fourteen years, when these people made themselves known to me, I would bring them to Patty for a session. Now that we were no longer living in the same state, I felt I should still find a way to help them.

☙

Here are some examples of how troubled people are brought to my attention.

I was sitting at the edge of a public pool in a completely unfamiliar city, watching my young daughter swim, and was approached by a perfect stranger. A lady, younger than me, came over and sat down next to me. She opened with talk about Irishness. She made the assumption based on my looks. I didn't really say much of anything. Irishness led her to speaking about her husband who must have had similar coloring to mine, which led to her telling me about their abusive marriage and recent divorce, which led to her pointing out her young redheaded son. That led to her expressing concerns about anxiety and other fear-related symptoms her son had been having, and oh by the way, the new house they were renting was obviously haunted. I had the whole story in less than five minutes, and I had never even told her anything about myself other than, "I do alternative healing."

Since I didn't know her at all, I gave her my card and some quick instructions on how she and her son could claim their space. I also gave her a little talk about how trauma acts like a magnet, and suggested by working out her own internalized trauma, she would be providing protection to her son.

Here's another one.

An old friend called after we had been out of touch several years. She didn't know what I'd been up to all this time. We were catching up on old times. She had suffered significant health struggles, having been hospitalized and in a coma two years ago. She was explaining the severe domestic problems she was having with her partner, and how she had already come up with an extreme solution to end the problems. She was going to transfer her job to another state, sell her house, offer her domestic partner a financial settlement and move without him. She couldn't figure out what else to do.

When I heard this, I asked her a few questions – "Has life changed dramatically since you were in a coma two years ago?"

She explained their drinking was out of control and they were becoming estranged from everyone they knew. Even her mother and siblings had begun to treat them differently. I asked another question. "Does your partner drink so much alcohol, it seems like it would kill the average person?"

I could hear her in the background gasping, "Oh my God!" She said to me, "Yes."

Then I began to explain how spirit attachment works. Regarding her partner, I explained that often the spirit of a deceased alcoholic person will go to a bar, and latch onto someone who is drinking their favorite drink. Then the host, who only used to go out on Friday nights, is suddenly drinking vast quantities every day. According to Dr. Edith Fiore in <u>The Unquiet Dead</u>, when a spirit is attached to a host, it can feel about 1/3 the "buzz" the host is feeling, and will encourage him to drink more and more so it can get "wasted." Meanwhile the host is consuming dangerous quantities of alcohol. He is arguing with obnoxious spirits who clamor in his head until he goes straight to the bottle. This can happen with drugs and food, as well.

She became very excited. "This is a MIRACLE! What amazing TIMING that we should talk now, after all these years! My partner claimed just the other night someone sat down on the couch next to him and was moving the couch back and forth, but no one was there. I thought he was hallucinating. His personality has changed completely. He is unable to hold a job, and his family doesn't want anything to do with him. We don't sleep in the same room anymore. Even when he's sound asleep, he's cursing and swearing! I wondered if he was possessed…"

She had become obsessed with watching paranormal TV shows, in hopes of finding an answer. On some level, she *knew* the source of her daily nightmare was paranormal in nature. When I made it clear I thought she might also have spirits attached to her, she was filled with fears and questions. She wondered if it might be her Dad attached to her, and if he was, did she really want to send him away? Then she brought up a miscarriage she had sustained about 25 years ago. She was really having a lot of angst about it, even after all this time. Inability to complete the grief cycle is a big red flag. If you lose a baby and are still grieving after 25 years, odds are good the spirit of the baby has never left you.

I told her I felt strongly she had brought someone home with her from the hospital. As I say, she had "company." And because the two of them have been drinking vast quantities of alcohol for years, it is probable they had taken on spirits long before she went into the hospital. It becomes a vicious cycle, as you take on someone else's symptoms and addictions, your vibrational frequency becomes lower and lower, you get sicker and sicker and, pretty soon, you can't stop more alcoholic, low-energy entities from getting on board. Her partner had become what I call "a party boat." He was having panic attacks, paranoia, and was completely unable to hold a job or function in daily life. They were going to lose the house.

She wanted me to come across the country and visit right away. She was willing to cover airfare. Even in their case, of advanced alcoholism and seemingly significant mental illness, I felt very hopeful they could turn their lives around if they could get rid of all those spirits. Then at least, they'd only have their own addictions and symptoms to deal with, and it wouldn't seem so overwhelming. That's the gist of it. Get it down to just you.

Unfortunately, these folks were too suspicious to try my simple technique. When I checked in a year later, I found that her now estranged partner had consumed so much alcohol, he had destroyed his liver. At age 48, he was in a care facility, on a waiting list for a liver transplant. She said, "We were together ten years. The first eight were great, but the last two years were absolute hell." Those last two years were after she had been in the coma... It was too late for him, but again I encouraged her to try reading out loud the statements I had sent her. She said. "It's the weirdest thing – I lose everything. I have no memory anymore. I can receive something in the mail, put it somewhere and never find it again." That is a classic sign of spirit attachment. When a visiting spirit is controlling your body in a time of intoxication, the host will have no recollection what was said or done during that time. And the alcohol always gets the blame.

Here's a third example.

A woman and her husband walked into my office one day, when I was working a regular job. I thought they had come for business reasons. Within a few moments, they were explaining her physical problems to me. For decades she had been suffering from nausea, digestive distress, fatigue, low grade fever and depression, and after four unsuccessful exploratory abdominal surgeries searching for the cause, the doctors were now suggesting a fifth surgery. She really didn't want to have another surgery.

Why were they telling me all this? I didn't know them. Should I divulge my sideline while in the workplace? I could get fired, perhaps, if word got out about my special abilities. But here they were, telling me all their intimate details, as if by sacred design. What made them think they should come here and tell *me*? I couldn't help myself.

I explained the concept of spirit attachment, suggesting she may have been invaded during one of her many surgeries by the spirit of a sick person who had died in the hospital. She wanted me to come and clear her as soon as possible. In the meantime, I gave her the Claim Your Space instructions and recipe for the hot salt bath and sent her on her way. Salt has a very purifying effect and, used in conjunction with verbal expression of your intent to claim your space, seems to dislodge foreign energies. A week later, she called to tell me the results of her claiming her space and taking the hot salt bath. After repeating the assigned phrases, she became nauseous. Per my recommendation, she continued making the statements, even though she felt ill. She developed a fever, so she took the hot salt bath and went to bed. The important thing was, she didn't give up.

During the night, she remembered being in the hospital twenty years previously, for an emergency C-section. She had been wheeled into a hallway on a gurney, and came to rest next to a female patient in critical condition. My client said she thought the woman was already dead, but she was experiencing peritonitis after a ruptured appendix. There was only one operating room available, and the doctors decided the peritonitis patient needed attention first. The woman died during surgery. Due to the urgent nature of my client's pregnancy, she was brought into the operating room immediately after the other patient had died. She said they hadn't even cleaned the room first. She remembered feeling very fatigued after the delivery, and for months afterward, was preoccupied with the desire to die. Her family was alarmed that, with the new baby, she had such a strong desire to leave earthly life behind.

Now, twenty years later, she suddenly realized she must have had the spirit of the peritonitis victim attached to her all these years. It was the cause of her depression and all of her physical symptoms. She tailored her space claiming statements as if to address the dead woman directly. She told her to go to the Light, and the next morning, my client woke to feel better than she had in decades. I went to her home for a follow up and performed my hands on healing treatment, intending to clear her of any spirits that may still have been attached to her. By listening to the resonance of a bell along her shushumna, or core of light in front of the spine, to which the chakras are connected, I could tell there was a blockage in her second chakra, or lower abdominal, area. I continued clearing her energy bodies until the bell rang clear. Later, she looked absolutely radiant. She said her only regret was she hadn't known about claiming her space before agreeing to those four exploratory surgeries.

After fourteen years, I have come to attribute every nagging physical, mental and emotional problem a person is having to possible spirit attachment. I am not talking about commonplace infections, fleeting colds and things. I'm talking about mysterious situations that truly debilitate and disable people, diseases and conditions with or without names. Especially in cases where people don't seem to remember anything specific that caused the problem, and claim repeated trips to medical facilities have never gotten to the root of it.

Often the medical industry has named a disease or condition and can describe it, but they really don't know how it came about, or how to get it to go away. They throw drugs and surgery at it, and send you to a psychiatrist or on your way home… If you've ever had a doctor say to you, "Well, you have all the symptoms of blah-de-blah, but I can't find any cause," suspect spirit attachment. If you have ever had surgery and have felt not-quite-the-same since, suspect spirit attachment. If you've been to a doctor repeatedly, complaining of very specific symptoms, only to have the doctor say, "Perhaps it's time I referred you to a Psychiatrist" *please* suspect spirit attachment.

One odd indication of spirit attachment is while you may be exhibiting real symptoms, your actual blood tests and other lab results can come back normal. That's when the doctor, for lack of any evidence, lumps you into the "psychosomatic" category. And if you follow your doctor's instructions and go see a psychiatrist, you add, to your already burdened system, the further debilitation of pharmaceutical effects and side effects. Now your human energy field is burdened with your pre-existing symptoms, the symptoms belonging to someone else, *and* the symptoms of being drugged every day. It can feel like an impossible dilemma.

ଔ

When I'm on a case, I'm completely focused. There isn't any place else I'd rather be. Yet, there I was on my 45th birthday, facing my angry young son, wondering if he was right. I already felt pretty worthless, not bringing in any income. And I wasn't quite fitting in with the locals. So, I decided, "He's right. Maybe I am wasting my time. From this moment forward, I will not spend another minute preoccupying myself with ghosts and helping people in my weird way. As of this moment, I am trashing my website (that I had spent a month building but hadn't yet launched), and focusing my efforts on being a 'normal' wife and mother. I thought to myself, if anyone asks me if I have any hobbies, I'll say, 'knitting.' I'm not going to talk or think about spirit attachment. If the Universe really wants me to do this work, **I am going to need obvious signs**. I am not seeking it out ANYMORE!"

I recently found a notebook, from 1996, when I had been sitting with my spiritual teacher, Leslie Temple-Thurston of CoreLight. She said, "If you seek it, it's opportunistic. If it falls in your lap, it's Grace." Profit from the work had never landed in my lap, but the work itself, unusual as it is, falls into my lap almost daily...

I didn't have to wait long for a sign. The day after my birthday I was moving around the house, trying to be more present and more productive than usual, when the phone rang. It was someone calling me for a perfectly normal and benign reason. She was responding about a potluck we had scheduled, and was trying to decide what she would bring. We talked about that for a minute. Then *she* brought up Reiki, a form of hands-on energy healing I am certified to provide. I had recently offered her a free Reiki treatment following her surgery. I told her it would clear the anesthesia-induced toxins out of her liver and help her body to heal more quickly. But she seemed reluctant, so I let it go.

On the phone she was saying, "My friend got a video about Reiki. I want to see what it's all about before I have a treatment. I'm a little leery about someone "putting energy in me" because, when we were little, we got attacked by demons… a lot."

My antennae were up immediately. What would be the best question to ask her first? *"Was it associated with a particular place?"*

"Yeah, in the house where we grew up."

I couldn't help myself. I blurted it out. "I've been afraid to tell anyone, but I do healing work in the area of spirit attachment!" I went on to explain a few general concepts to her.

This lady and I had met when we were signing our kids up for summer sports. She had told me she belonged to a specific church, and had said she didn't believe in "spirits and all that." She had also told me, on a different occasion, for many years, one of her beautiful sisters had suffered from a rare disorder that involved constantly picking at the skin on her face. She had been to numerous doctors, and been put on various medications. When she told me of this, my immediate thought was the girl had a spirit attached to her. But I didn't say anything. If there was a spirit attached to her who didn't recognize itself when she looked in the mirror, the spirit might attempt to take off the "mask" (her face) hiding its "real" face. There have been many documented cases like it. (See Dr Carl Wickland's, Thirty Years Among the Dead).

Now here we were, a few months later, and she's telling me she and her siblings were possessed by demons when she was young! Maybe I *was* right about her sister. But this wasn't your standard topic of conversation, and usually not thrown in with decisions about a potluck! After our conversation ended, I felt encouraged. Perhaps I was still a divining rod after all.

Not thirty minutes had passed when the phone rang again. It was a woman in the Bay Area, responding to our ad in the Share Guide. We'd had so few responses in the seven months since we placed the ad I had completely forgotten we placed it at all. But here, on the day I needed a sign, was a woman who needed help.

She said, "I had a nine-hour surgery in April, and I haven't felt right since."

I counted the months that had passed since April – seven - in my head, and said, "That's a long time (for not bouncing back). Do you feel fatigued?"

"Yes, very."

I asked, "Did you come out with symptoms you didn't have when you went in?

"Yes! And lately I've found myself thinking, 'I wonder if I'm dead?' I don't know why I would be thinking that, because it's obvious I'm not dead."

Jackpot. I said, trying not to be too enthusiastic, "That's not you. You are hearing somebody else's thoughts. A spirit probably got attached to you while you were having surgery. It's very common. When you are put under general anesthesia, the poison pushes you out of your body. As they say at the psychic institute, when you check out, you leave the door open. The combination of being put under anesthesia and having your body cut open makes you very vulnerable to spirit attachment. Hospitals and operating rooms are full of spirits, and when they die under anesthesia or while in a coma, they get confused, not realizing they are dead, and often they don't go to the Light.

"Say an elderly woman died during surgery in the same operating room, right before you went in, and, being confused and not sure she had died, she entered your body during your procedure. You might find yourself thinking, 'Wow, I feel old," or you may crave foods and drinks you didn't like before. You can also take on their symptoms. You might feel fatigued, achy, or suddenly have thoughts are not your own."

She said, "Normally I would never go in for this spirit stuff, but things haven't been right for some time, and I realized this is what I might be dealing with. Everything you say seems to make sense."

I gave her the recipe for the hot salt bath and the words to the Claim Your Space Exercise. I stressed how important it is to do the clearing out loud so the spirit can hear it. I recommended she do the clearing exercise every day for a week, and do it in the bath at least once. I told her I felt confident it would work because the spirit already realizes something is wrong. I told her, since she feels confident someone else is in her body, she could tailor the talk more specifically.

The woman, whose name I never even got, thanked me profusely and said she would do everything I recommended. I told her to call me back in a week if she felt it didn't work. I never heard from her again. After that conversation, my adrenaline was pumping, and I was a little light headed. It HAD to be a sign, number two, in less than an hour.

For the rest of the day, I was thinking cynically, "I wonder if I should add the stipulation that there should be three occurrences, since my mother always told me things happen in threes?" I didn't realize until the next day I DID have a third occurrence.

ଔ

In between those two wonderful phone calls, I had been online, exchanging emails with the lady who had posted a blog about her young son having an invisible playmate, and a ghost he said was trying to "get" him. She explained this activity had begun when they moved into the house a year earlier. This kind of conversation had become second nature to me, so I didn't think to count it as the third sign until the next day.

Here is an excerpt of that conversation:

"We have lived in this house for 15 months. My son never spoke of imaginary friends until we moved here. After we were here for three months, my son started speaking of "Billy and his cat." My son will wake in the middle of the night, come into my room and say, "Billy told the ghost to go away but the ghost is bugging me...can I sleep with you?" He will ask, "Can Billy sit on your bed, Mommy?" and then turn and speak to Billy as if he was a real person. In my son's mind, I can see Billy too. He is so matter of fact about Billy and very sure there is a ghost, it is interrupting his sleep.

"My older son swears something has grabbed him while he was walking down the hall...and in the very same spot, I did hear something say in my ear, "Get out"! I of course replied, "I will not!" And since then, I have not heard anything, but can still feel a presence.... Even my mom, who isn't into ghosts, said something about the feeling in this house. I told it I don't mind if it stays, but I don't want it to harm or make contact with my family."

"We know the ghost is an old man. He stays in the stairwell and the hallway. He will sometimes go into my younger son's room...I assume it is the ghost that is upsetting him. My son is highly intelligent...not your normal 5 year old child. My older son is 18 and is very bothered by the presence in the house, and says he hears things in his closet."

What usually happens is our dialogue on the blog post becomes so personal they choose to email me privately and we continue the process like that. Over the course of a few email exchanges, she had pretty much figured it out on her own. On the day in question - the day after my birthday - she was emailing to thank me for my compassion and gentle explanations, and to say she was going to try my recommendations.

That was my third sign in just a few hours... and my son thinks I don't do anything all day! I thanked Spirit for the obvious clues and concluded, I guess I can't give it up after all!

A few months later, I received follow up from the lady above. As a courtesy, she sent me a little message. Here it is.

"Since I met you and did what you told me, my son hasn't spoken of "Billy" in his room and our home and life have been in total harmony and peace for at least 2 solid months! It hasn't been this wonderful in years… until I met you! And I mean that with all my heart. You are so awesome and I just love all you speak of. You have helped me in so many ways, you just don't know!! Well, maybe you do?"

This is why I can't leave this work behind. This is why I have written this book. These Claim Your Space methods really work and are mind bogglingly simple to do.

The Vortex of Hell

"There is a form of energy that is a product of life processes, probably best described as 'auric energy' and this energy naturally accumulates, bounded by physical objects. As such, any place that has had long-time human occupancy and/or the expression of extreme emotion is apt to have ample energy of the kind necessary for etheric-to-physical influences to occur."

The American Association of Electronic Voice Phenomena www.aaevp.com.

I consider myself a haunted house survivor. I grew up in a house that was built circa 1720, and know firsthand how hellish it is to be stuck in a house thick with accumulated energies. My childhood home was an extremely haunted house on the East coast, and it very nearly destroyed my family. Not all of us got out of the house alive. I refer to the house as the Vortex of Hell.

Even though we sold the house in 1983, Patty and I did a distance clearing on the house in 2000, on behalf of anyone who had ever set foot there, so they would be spared the horrors we experienced within those walls. Since I moved out and began to heal my life, all things have pointed me toward the realization that spirit interference is a significant cause of human ills. It has now become my heart's desire to free others as I have learned to free my family members and myself.

Twenty-two years after we sold the house, my husband and I were chatting with my sister and brother-in-law about punctuality. We were comparing notes about how we each operate, and what our priorities are regarding time. Sis's husband liked to wait until the very last minute to get to his appointments, or he felt he had wasted time. My sister confessed she liked to get up very early to prepare, and even reach her appointments ahead of schedule. My husband has no problem getting to his appointments well in advance.

I found myself going back in my memory, to life on High Street. I commented, even though we had lived two minutes from the elementary school, I had never been able to get to school on time. We were so close to the campus, I could practically hit the school with a rock. My sister piped up, saying the family referred to my Mother as "the late" Mrs. Kiernan. She couldn't get anywhere on time either. I had said it felt so bad to be late for class, eventually I didn't want to go to school anymore.

When my husband asked why I couldn't get to school on time, I said, "Because while we were in that house, it was like being stuck in a time warp. We were trapped in the Vortex of Hell."

My sister murmured, "Yeah, the Vortex of Hell."

As I write this, I realize the glue that keeps you trapped in a haunted house is the same glue that keeps you in an abusive relationship or in dysfunctional behavior patterning. When you're on the outside looking in, you may think, why doesn't she just *leave* (the abusive relationship or the house), or why doesn't she just *pull herself together* (and stop staying in a self destructive situation)? What outsiders don't realize is, it isn't easy to get out. It's like being stuck in a vortex. A vortex spins, like one of those centrifugal rides at the carnival where you get pinned to the wall, and you can't move, even though the floor drops out from under you. You can breathe, but you can't seem to get free of the force. You can barely function, and the scenario continues as if it has a life of its own. You're sure you can do nothing but stand paralyzed in fear until it's over. You feel as if your life is in jeopardy, and it may well be, and you can only think from second to second, or freeze in the paralysis of fear and helplessness as the spinning continues.

I learned from my enlightened teacher, Leslie Temple Thurston of Corelight, human life has a default setting of duality. Night/day, male/female, victim/tyrant - the permutations are endless. These polar opposites of experience set us into a spin. It's what makes the world go around, for us humans. She also refers to it as drama. When you're caught in the drama of being in an abusive relationship or living in a haunted house, you really feel as if you can't escape. You're completely enveloped in a pattern. There's no perspective on the inside.

I have concluded traumatic events create karmic and supernatural phenomena. They set up the victim/tyrant spin. Without realizing it, we become the tornado, and attract similar events to us. In addition to our personal spin, I now believe certain places have a spin of their own, due to an accumulation of trauma energy. And those places attract people of similar vibration to it. If you have an Irish American set of parents with early childhood abandonment issues, who come from a culture that had been oppressed, enslaved and abused for centuries, with the trauma of World War 2 still fresh in their hearts and minds, they might be, unwittingly of course, a perfect match for the larger vortex of the haunted house. Their energies match. They get sucked into the familiar energy, and perhaps cannot get out.

When you're caught up in the spin, it may seem impossible to escape, but there is a way out. It reminds me of the instructions the lifeguards give you when you get caught in an undertow at the ocean. Don't try to swim against it, swim out the side. If you go with it, you will drown. If you swim against it, you will exhaust yourself and drown. Swimming with it or against it are the polar opposites. Swimming out the side is the middle way and saves your life. It gets you out of the default setting. One minute you're in a situation that feels like it has no solution, and the next minute, you're treading water right next to the teeming whirlpool that almost caused your demise. You're in the same ocean, almost in the same spot, but the circumstances are now completely different. You're floating in a sea of calm. You almost can't believe you were just in a treacherous situation. It all seems almost unreal.

The Claim Your Space™ techniques show you how to swim out the side of the undertow, to get out of the spin by finding the middle way. The tools are very simple, yet profoundly effective, and may very well save your life. They can be applied to clearing your human energy field of spirits as well as the residue of trauma. You can use the same tools to begin to eliminate deep emotional issues, as well as clearing unpleasant situations you encounter in daily life. You can use them preventively, just in case, when you know you are going to be put under general anesthesia, for instance, or going to a funeral. These exercises can be incorporated into your daily life, like washing your hands or brushing your teeth.

As I said earlier, once a traumatic event occurs in your life, it sets you up in the victim/tyrant spin. As spirit clearers, we discovered trauma is like a magnet, drawing similar experiences to it. If an event occurred causing one person or several people to feel frightened for their lives, violated and betrayed, the energy will linger in that spot long after the murderous event has been forgotten. Another group of people comes along, and soon they're engaged in a scenario that seems to have a plan of its own. Soon, they're experiencing terrible fear, violation and betrayal. Someone may even die.

The pattern takes hold and similar actions are heaped on, generation after generation. That's how you can end up with a phenomenon like a haunted house, or a severely damaged human being who is stuck in the hell of unhealthy patterning.

ଔ

Our house had a reputation long before we arrived. When a sensitive person feels another person or a place is "creepy," I think they are detecting the thick energy of trauma described as auric energy in the introduction to this chapter. The sign hanging on the front of the house says circa 1720, but Mom always insisted the house was much older. It is impossible to trace the absolute origin of what became my home because my mother always told me there was no original deed to the house– only a Bill of Sale for a pre-existing structure. She assumed, in 1720, the original owner sold the house to the second owner, so it's anyone's guess when the house was actually built. (Oddly, my mother was so determined the house was older, she would never accept the 1720 date offered by Town officials. The next owners gladly accepted the circa sign after we sold the house.)

We occupied it for thirty years between 1953 and 1983. At some point in the three hundred years before we moved into our family home, an initial trauma must have taken place on the property or in the house. I think it happened on the land, before the house was built. Then for generations, the magnetic effect caused more events like it to take place until the house was thick with traumatic experience. Let's look at what might have started the spin leading to the violence and tragedy of my family's life on High Street.

My childhood home was in a town called Huntington, on Eastern Long Island. My siblings found Indian paint pots and arrowheads in the hillside next to the driveway for decades. While there, my father and brothers developed a very strong interest in and preoccupation with "being" Indians. My father made a very elaborate chieftain's headdress, with dozens of feathers going all the way down the wearer's back. He made deerskin outfits for the boys. He bought a small loom and spent hours weaving Indian style beaded belts and accessories. They used the real paint pots they found in the yard to paint stripes on their faces and danced around in the driveway with tomahawks. One brother nearly split the other's skull, accidentally of course, with the tomahawk. That's the problem with a pre-existing magnetic pull. Things happen. My father took them to the Pow Wows on the Shinnecock Reservation out on Montauk Point. I don't know why we didn't realize we were being influenced while it was happening, but looking back it sure seems obvious.

**Headdress like the one my father made, left.
Natives of Long Island, circa 1905, right.**

Years later when I was growing up and the paint pots and arrowheads were all gone, I, too, developed a significant interest in the Native American lifestyle. When I was ten years old, I had vivid recurring fantasies about being a squaw dressed in deerskin and moccasins, padding fearfully through the snow on a quiet winter day. I never saw what I was running or hiding from in those fantasies, but something was going to get me if I wasn't very quiet. My heart would pound and I would try my best to be invisible, even though there's not a lot of foliage to hide behind in the winter. It felt like the pressure would never let up. A traditional therapist might say it was anxiety, fear of the unknown, and was triggered by some unrelated stressor in my life at the time. But what if it was exactly what I saw? What if I was caught up in the energy pervading the property on which I lived? So often, we are led off the track by well-meaning but limited thinkers.

There were several times in my childhood when I had that same feeling of needing to be very quiet. While in bed, I would hear creaky noises that sounded exactly like someone was creeping up the stairs and toward my room to "get" me. I would slowly get out of my bed, pick up a tennis racket and stand in the closet, racket overhead, waiting and waiting for the intruder to enter my room. I was afraid to breathe too loudly in case it heard me. But there was nothing I could do about the pounding of my heart.

I used to cry in indignation at the popular Western shows on TV while I was growing up. The feelings of robbed innocence and senseless victimization pervaded our lives and made me feel very sad, most of my childhood.

Because the midden heap of discarded Indian goods was literally right outside our back door, I made the assumption our house may have been built on top of an Indian village. I'm guessing there could have been violence and murder involved in the changeover from Native settlement to a white man's home. It is interesting, the founding date of the town, 1653, is only ten years after the Dutch and Indian War on Long Island, when at least a thousand Indians were massacred and the survivors began a mass exodus. Here is an excerpt from my hometown's local newspaper, The Long Islander.

"Most of the early settlers were English people who came to Huntington by way of Massachusetts and Connecticut. As a result, they felt more of a kinship with New England than with their Dutch neighbors to the west in New Amsterdam. The town in fact voted in 1660 to place itself under the jurisdiction of Connecticut to gain some protection from the Dutch."

All three cultures, English, Dutch and Native American, were in direct competition for the fertile lands of Long Island. The new immigrants had ruthless solutions for getting rid of the native population. So perhaps the area was vacant when construction began on our house, but the violence and terror of the massacres and forced exodus could easily have lingered.

When my sister went to a psychic in England sometime in the 1970's, she was told she had an 'Indian' guide, a male. She never made the connection between that information and the fact that we had been raised on top of an old Indian dwelling. One séance conducted in our front room in 1982 produced an angry Native American spirit who said he was a guardian of the land where our house was built.

Here are more excerpts from my hometown's local newspaper, The Long Islander.

"In 1640, as other Englishmen and their families began to move in small groups to the eastern end of Long Island, the Dutch continued to buy up the west end. There were political reasons for the Dutch's aggressive land purchases, which displaced hundreds of Indians. In addition to finding pastureland, the Dutch needed to push settlements into Long Island as a counterbalance to the growing English presence on the East End. The Dutch could not allow the English to take it all, so they knew they had to claim as much of the west end of the island as they could. But the Dutch also knew they couldn't stop the English from setting up villages on the East End, so the island essentially became both Dutch and English at the same time."

"Governor Kieft's War, 1640 to 1645, resulted in the deaths of more than one thousand Native Americans and a few dozen whites. In 1643, warfare between Dutch settlers and Indians spilled across the region. Some of the Indians in western Long Island may have fled east. Hundreds of others looked west for safety. The Dutch expanded their settlements onto the western end of Long Island, pushing aside the Delaware and turning them into refugees."

"The Delaware fled the region of the lower Hudson River and western Long Island in the early 1640s to escape certain

extinction in a war waged by Dutch settlers. The English arrived on the East End in the late 1630s.

"The Rev. Isaac Jogues, a Jesuit priest from France, was murdered by Indians in 1646. He was the first Catholic missionary to work in what is now New York State, and he was the first to be martyred. Before he was killed, missionary Jogues wrote a brief account of what he witnessed between August 1643, and November 1644, the atrocities of the Dutch-Indian wars. His keen eye during the 10 months he lived at New Amsterdam provides readers today with an extraordinary look at a troubled time and place."

"Of the bloodshed that spilled across the Lower Hudson River Valley and into western Long Island, Jogues wrote: 'Some (Indian) nations near the sea having murdered some Hollanders of the most distant settlement, the Hollanders killed 150 Indians, men, women and children ... And in the beginning of winter the grass being low and some snow on the ground they pursued them with six hundred men, keeping two hundred always on the move and constantly relieving each other, so that the Indians, pent up in a large island and finding it impossible to escape, on account of women and children, were cut to pieces to the number of sixteen hundred, women and children included. This obliged the rest of the Indians to make peace, which still continues. This occurred in 1643 and 1644.'

Another story - "By the winter of 1643, relations between the Dutch and their Indian neighbors had gone bad. Suddenly, there were killings on both sides and calls for war. Willem Kieft, Dutch official in charge at New Amsterdam, decided an attack on the Indian villages should come when the men were off hunting.

"The "design" -- as the attack plan was called -- was executed Feb. 25, 1643, with Dutch soldiers attacking an encampment less than a mile from New Amsterdam. Eighty Indians were killed and 30 taken prisoner.

"Of the attack by the Dutch, a book titled <u>A History of the City of Brooklyn</u>, published in 1867, said the Indians were *'remorselessly butchered ... The story of that night is one of the saddest and foulest upon the pages of New Netherland's history.' A Dutch account published in the mid-17th Century said '... young children were cut in pieces before the eyes of their parents, and the pieces were thrown into the fire or into the water; other babes were bound on planks and then cut through, stabbed and miserably massacred, so that it would break a heart of stone ..."'*

Our house was on the North shore, where the British sought after the land. The Brits fought the Dutch who already had Manhattan, and the Indians were right in the middle.

According to a book I read about the history of Huntington, one early inhabitant of our house was an English Captain. Even though it's hard to tell whether the above quoted events happened on or near my property, it lends an idea to the level of fear and violence pervading the entire island at the time. That kind of horror has a lingering effect. Not to mention what I now take for granted, when persons die suddenly (by murder or what have you) they often do not realize they have died. It can be the beginning of a haunting. Add to that desire for revenge, which anyone would feel after watching their babies being butchered, as well as the guilt felt by the perpetrators, and you have lots of tormented spirits hanging around, interfering with the living, and keeping the patterning of trauma in place.

Later, our house had been a homestead, the main house on a large farm. The property stretched vast in all directions. In fact, for some unknown reason, people who frequented our house while we lived there began referring to it as "the Homestead." The psychic determined there had been slaves and unconsecrated bodies in the basement in previous centuries. Either the killing took place in there, or bodies were put there. She felt the energy of slaves, aborted, miscarried or unbaptized babies, and at least one murder victim. The energy she picked up on could also have been the intense emotions felt by the slaves who might have been in captivity in the basement. Until she mentioned slaves being in our house, during the psychic healing session in 2000, I had never before considered that reality. So I did some research.

More quotes from the Long Islander.

"Slavery in New York was quite different from the plantation slavery we often imagine," writes Marcus. "Few New Yorkers owned vast numbers of slaves. The rare Long Island farmer with a dozen or so slaves probably housed them in slave cabins separate from the main house. **But slave owners with only one or two slaves might have them living in an attic, a cellar or some other out-of-the-way section of their own homes.**

"While the Dutch took an almost casual approach to the treatment and control of the slaves that were imported into the colony after 1626, **everything changed after the British took over in 1664. The British, who controlled what was now New York, not only stepped up the importation of slaves into America, they passed a series of slave codes regulating slavery that made it harsher, repressive and more brutal."**

"As the colonial period came to an end, on the eve of the Revolutionary War, slavery remained a potent force on Long Island. **According to a 1755 census, there were 81 slaves belonging to 35 families in Huntington."**

The spin was well in place by then. Slaves were being victimized daily, and over generations. One might think, "How can one human being do this to another?" Unresolved victim issues, like ongoing slavery and torture, produce tyrannical behavior. There was no middle way, only opposing extremes. We have found victimized spirits tend to stay in the earth plane, hoping to exact an explanation or apology from their murderers. At the same time, the perpetrators, or tyrants, also get stuck in the moment, by guilt, remorse and fear they won't be allowed into Heaven. And the victim/tyrant scenario continues to play out.

And of course, we cannot forget, Long Island was a hotbed of activity during the Revolutionary War. Our house stood during that violent reign. There's a statue of Nathan Hale in a part of Huntington, and the area was named Halesite. Here is a quote from the Town of Huntington website, http://town.huntington.ny.us/town_history.cfm.

"In June 1774 Huntington adopted a "Declaration of Rights" affirming "that every freeman's property is absolutely his own" and that taxation without representation is a violation of the rights of British subjects. The Declaration of Rights also called for the colonies to unite in a refusal to do business with Great Britain. Two years later, news of the Declaration of Independence was received with great enthusiasm in Huntington, but the euphoria was short-lived. Following the defeat of the rebel forces at the Battle of Long Island on August 27, 1776, Long Island was occupied by the British Army. Residents were required to take oaths of allegiance to the Crown. **If a man refused to take the oath, he and his family could be turned off their property, losing everything.** *In 1782 the occupying army established an encampment in Huntington's Old Burying Ground, razing tombstones to clear the site. Not surprisingly, many townspeople resisted, waging guerilla warfare until the war was over and the British left in 1783.* (Rebellion against authority is another aspect of the victim/tyrant polarity.)

Nathan Hale landed at Huntington in 1776, coming by boat from Norwalk, Connecticut, on a spying mission for George Washington. Sent to gather information about the British forces on Long Island and in New York City, he was captured and executed in New York City in September 1776. A memorial stands at the approximate site of his coming ashore in Huntington, an area now known as Halesite."

In our town, the victim/rebel was the hero, but was crushed by the authorities. Since our house was standing in 1776, no doubt it was put to use by whatever forces were in the area. Because it was large, it could have housed many troops. One can only imagine the trauma-producing activities that might have taken place at our house during the Revolutionary period. Our family lived constantly in fear of being made to leave the house. For us, the reasons were economic, but the energy was still the same. Shame and anger were the predominant emotions. Our feelings matched those of the colonists in the Revolutionary War period as well as the slaves and natives who were forced to flee.

☙

Fast forward, a hundred years from the time of the Revolution. Part of a well-documented tragedy, named the Kelsey Outrage, took place on November 4, 1872, on or very near our property in Huntington. This was only 80 years before we moved in. The incident had such an impact the town was nicknamed "Tar Town." The famous tarring and feathering incident had been committed on Main Street, as a way to get rid of an unpopular man who was infatuated with a young local woman.

It really was a set up, since on previous occasions, he had been invited into the bedroom window of a certain young lady, by the light of a lamp. It is unclear whether the girl tired of the man, or whether her newfound love interest wanted to harm him. On this unfortunate evening, when he responded to the lamplight, upon climbing into his girlfriend's bed he found himself groping the breast of her Aunt. She let out a scream and the men, who were waiting nearby, pounced on him, torturing him viciously before he finally bled to death. The framing and murder of the man Charles Kelsey traumatized every citizen in the town of Huntington. It could easily be likened to the remorseless butchering of the Native Indians more than two hundred years before, right down to the detail of someone being cut into pieces and their body parts being thrown into the water.

"The assailants threw Kelsey to the ground, roughly cut his hair and beard and stripped him naked. After covering his body with hot tar, they dumped feathers over him, and exhibited him to the women who had gathered outside. Then

released, he staggered up Spring Street to the house he shared with his sister, Charlotte. (From Main Street, that would have been toward our house.) *From that point on, Kelsey was missing.*

"The day after the tar-and-feathering, a fisherman found a blood-soaked shirt, a necktie and two lemons on the shore at Lloyd Neck, looking out over Cold Spring Harbor.

"The story was picked up by newspapers and spread far and wide. Huntington became known as "Tar Town." Residents lined up in two opposing factions, with the "Tars" supporting the punishment of Kelsey, the "Anti-Tars" opposing it. (victim/tyrant polarity)

"On Aug. 29, 1873, two men fishing in Oyster Bay Harbor between Moses Point and Plum Point spotted the lower half of what turned out to be Kelsey floating in the water. The legs were encased in a pair of black pants which were later identified as probably Kelsey's, and attached to the pants was a gold watch chain that was identified as his. On cutting off the trousers, tar and feathers were found still on the legs. The genitals had been hacked off.

"A coroner's inquest in Oyster Bay began building a case. Doctors testified Kelsey had been alive when mutilated, and that he died from blood loss due to the emasculation. On Oct. 25, 1873, the coroner's jury concluded Kelsey had been murdered, but it did not specify by whom. On November 7, 1873, two men were indicted for the murder of Charles Kelsey. (November 7th happens to be my birthday.)

My mother always told me an elderly woman came to our door one day, claiming she had lived in our house when she was a child. She arrived in a chauffeur-driven car, and claimed to be a member of the offending family, who was responsible for Mr. Kelsey's murder. If she came to the door in the 1960's and was aged in her 90s, then that would have put her occupying the house right round the time of the murder of Charles Kelsey. Why would this elderly lady feel compelled to return to the property so many decades later? It caused me to wonder if, during the time Mr. Kelsey was considered missing, he may have been brought to the property of the offending family before finally meeting his demise – to our house. Perhaps she had been a witness to part of the heinous crime. Perhaps a sense of guilt brought her back to the scene. Or perhaps she was caught up in the "spin" of an early childhood trauma that remained unresolved in her psyche.

ଓଃ

During our tenure in the house, between 1953 and 1983, there was a seemingly endless swirl of situations in which my family felt victimized, ostracized and unwelcome. I will highlight two incidents which occurred with similar energy to the 'lynch mob' or tarring and feathering mentality. I will recount the later one first, since it was the less intense of the two examples.

My mother had always struggled to support her five children after my father left, substituting teaching for many school districts. One day in 1978, there was an opportunity to sub in a Catholic school district while the teachers were on strike. My mother's decision to take the job, as a way to feed her children, was a source of outrage and shame for her friend, who had a Union job and felt like my mother was undermining an important cause. But my mother had strong loyalty to the Catholic Church, having been raised by nuns in a boarding school convent, so she was prepared to 'turn the other cheek,' and cross the picket line for the sake of the Church. One day, after my mother had taught at the Catholic school, unbeknownst to her, strikers followed her home. The next day while she was teaching again, our house was vandalized.

When I got home from high school, I found someone had smeared fecal matter all over our back porch, on the walls, windows and on my bicycle seat. When I went in the house, I could hear water running. I ran out to find a basement window had been broken and the vandals had put the hose in the basement and turned it on full blast. By the time I discovered it, there were several inches of water down there. My mother said we had sustained thousands of dollars worth of damage.

Later, since no legal charges had been filed, the Diocese offered my family a scholarship at the private Catholic high school. How ironic, I thought. I was the only child young enough to take advantage of their offer and I only had one year of high school left to go before I graduated. I spent my senior year attending a Catholic high school, so my mother could feel sufficiently compensated.

The event was frightening for the whole family, and we wondered how far the vandals would go. Would they come back and throw bricks in our windows, or hurt my mother by damaging her car while she was in it? For my mother, the betrayal was deep because, presumably, the people who had vandalized our house had been 'good' Catholic teachers. My mother had been raised by 'good' Catholics, and I think the rude victimization shocked and saddened her deeply. Her ideals were shattered. In a sense, her innocence was robbed. Anytime a violation occurs, innocence is robbed. It is reminiscent of the peaceful life of the Indians being shattered by greedy colonists, and the love of Mr. Kelsey being made shameful by a jealous rich boy. We were all just trying to live our lives, yet kept getting caught up in something else.

ಬ

Due to a bizarre turn of events and an apparent set up much like the Kelsey case 100 years before, another event occurred which cost the life of my oldest brother, Sean.

Sean Kiernan, 22, Dies Suddenly

Sean Kiernan, 22 of Huntington, died suddenly at his home Wednesday May 30 of unknown causes pending an autopsy at the Suffolk County Medical Examiner's office.

He was born September 30, 1950 in East Orange, N.J., to John B. and Sheila Kiernan. He attended Woodbury Avenue School, Toaz Junior High School, Coindre Hall and Huntington High School and excelled in sports at school. He also liked to write and left a book of poetry, which is not now in the possession of his mother and which she would appreciate having returned to her.

Kiernan reposed at the M.A. Connell Funeral Home where Richard Irwin, an English teacher at Finley Junior High School, eulogized him. A mass of the resurrection was offered Saturday morning at St. Patrick's R.C. Church.

Besides his mother and father, he is survived by two sisters, Geraldine Kiernan Paju of New York City and the Bahamas, Mary Kelly Kiernan of the home address and two brothers, Sgt. Kerry Kiernan, United States Air Force, of Minot, North Dakota, and Michael of the home address.

There were many issues involved, but the similarity of his situation to the persecution vibration of the Kelsey Outrage is uncanny. Like Mr. Kelsey, my oldest brother had attracted the ire of the powers-that-be in Huntington. In his youth, my brother was the kind of person who rescued injured birds and squirrels, and wrote poetry about the pain of life. At the same time, he grew physically strong and angry at authority for what he perceived to be abuse of power at the hands of my father. He also turned to alcohol and drugs to numb the unbearable pain of living in such a cruel world. Even though he was a compassionate young man who came to the defense of his female peers who were being hurt and humiliated by their arrogant boyfriends, Sean wasn't considered a model citizen, and had accumulated a string of minor legal offenses by the time he was a legal adult. He was thoroughly mired in victim/tyrant patterning.

Friends and loved ones knew my brother to be a tender hearted, melancholy soul who had been tortured in childhood. By the age of 22, he had gone through years of self-imposed punishment as well, including punishment by the law. He was finally free of drugs and had recently landed a job. Things were looking up. But by a weird stroke of misfortune or vibrational patterning, he was falsely accused of a crime downtown and, seeing no alternative, ended his own life.

A friend had recently graduated from basic training. My brother broke his sobriety to take the young man out for a few beers. As they left the bar on New York Avenue, the young military graduate decided to show my brother some moves he had learned in basic. He grabbed my brother by the arm, turned and flipped him over his back, judo style. My brother went reeling backwards and crashed into a plate glass window of the then Radio Shack store. The window shattered as my brother fell into the display. The alarm went off, and people came out of the bar across the street, in time to see a shaved haired man pull my brother out of the broken glass. They ran.

The police were called, and witnesses claimed they recognized my brother but not the other young man. Because of my brother's prior arrests, the assumption was, they were attempting to burglarize the store. My brother, understanding the prevailing mentality, never went home. He went into hiding, but communicated with my mother by phone. He explained to her what happened. When the police came to the house, she explained to them what happened. The police said the storeowner was pressing charges. My mother pleaded with the storeowner, explaining it was an accident, but he refused to drop the charges. My brother was afraid to go back to prison. After three days of telephone negotiations and rising panic, he decided he would rather end his life than be falsely accused and go to prison for attempted burglary. He died on Memorial Weekend, 1973.

My brother felt persecuted, trapped. He feared for his life. The situation quickly spun out of his control. He was caught up in the spin and believed there was no way out. Considering the patterning, one might conclude the initial energy of trauma at the house drew yet another similar incident to it, and we were merely hapless players in a scene we didn't realize we were in. Looking back, how could we possibly have resisted the strong spin most likely initiated by massacre, oppression and attempted genocide; and then reinforced generation after generation with victim/tyrant patterning in the forms of slavery, war and local terrorism? Here we were, thinking we got a bargain in this big, rambling house. We had no idea we had fallen straight into the Vortex of Hell.

How Spirits Get Attached to Us

"The Human Energy Field is the manifestation of the universal energy that is intimately involved with human life. It can be described as a luminous body that surrounds and interpenetrates the physical body, emits its own characteristic radiation and is usually called the "aura." The auric field is a quantum leap deeper into our personality than is our physical body. It is at this level of our being that our psychological processes take place. The human energy field is the vehicle for all psychosomatic reactions. ***The physical body arises out of the energy field, thus an imbalance or distortion in this field will eventually cause a disease in the physical body that it governs. Therefore, healing distortions in the field will bring about healing in the physical body.***"

>Barbara Ann Brennan of Hands of Light, former NASA scientist and innovative energy healer.

One purpose of this book is to make it clear that there is an invisible side to your life. The invisible side includes what are known as light bodies, or subtle bodies of energy, as well as spirit bodies. We each have many bodies, with different frequencies. The physical body is the densest of all our bodies. It is the one everybody can see and feel. Even though we cannot see our light bodies, something is always happening in these bodies, and, any problems that occur in the light bodies eventually manifest in the physical. Once you have that awareness, your whole outlook changes on what causes illness and how to treat yourself. Rather than thinking that problems begin in your physical body, consider that the problems arise on an emotional or other level and manifest in your human energy field. I refer to these foreign manifestations as densities. This problem, unrecognized, grows until it is finally manifested in your physical body. Now what do you do?

The activity of spirits, or persons who no longer have bodies, is another thing that happens in the invisible realm. If I say *spirit* in lower case, I am referring to someone who is floating around without his or her body. When I am talking about spirituality, I may refer to *Spirit*, upper case, which is synonymous with the Source of All That Is, or Divinity. I have been made aware that spirits can and do remain in the realm of the living and attach themselves to the living. Intermingling of spirit bodies with the human energy fields of the living is problematic for all concerned. When a spirit gets caught in the human energy field of a living being, I call that condition spirit attachment. From a psychic perspective, an attachment is a density in one's human energy field. There are other kinds of densities, as well. As Barbara Brennan stated in the above quote, "an imbalance or distortion in the human energy field will eventually cause a disease in the physical body that it governs."

Trauma

The most common way for a density to get started is to experience some kind of trauma. This trauma can be caused by verbal, physical or sexual assault or other act of violence, a sudden accident or witnessing a traumatic event. The density it creates in the human energy field is magnetic. It creates or attracts similar experiences to it, until the density grows to the point of physical, mental or emotional manifestation, like little magnet shavings sticking to the big magnet until there is a big pile. Like attracts like. Over time, the density buildup puts a strain on your energy field, and it begins to malfunction. Once our vibrational body is compromised, we become more vulnerable to all kinds of ailments, including spirit attachment. We see the end result of this buildup as symptoms in the physical body.

Densities can be caused by traumatic experience and spirit attachment. And spirit attachment usually, but not always, happens because of trauma that happened to somebody else – namely the spirit that is too traumatized to go to the Light. Trauma has such an impact on a person it can stay with you from lifetime to lifetime and stays in the energetic portion of you that transcends the physical. This may be what the Eastern religions refer to as karma.

The "glue" that keeps the density in place is often an emotional component. The emotional component is what carries over, and it brings with it the imprint of the previous experience. It's all part of one big density. Take a person with a faulty thyroid, for example. He may feel sure he never experienced a trauma to the neck in this life. He may have experienced a traumatic birth which he cannot remember. Sometimes mothers choose not to tell their children about a traumatic birth, thinking they will spare the child feelings of guilt. But the intensity of the moment is registered in the emotional bodies of both mother and child at the trauma site and may later manifest as physical illness. Many cases of claustrophobia, asthma and perhaps thyroid malfunction may be discovered, under hypnosis, to be caused by birth trauma.

The trauma may have been due to the cause of death in a past life. A Buddhist would call that past life karma. If a person had died by hanging, or had been strangled, that would leave a density in the neck area. For example, if a person had committed suicide by hanging, the actual act would be traumatic, and the unresolved guilt, remorse or feelings of abandonment would keep the trauma in place. If a person was sentenced to death by hanging as opposed to having done it to himself, the combination of the physical trauma of the event, coupled with *rage* against inhumane punishment and *desire* for revenge, would cause an imprint in the consciousness of that person, and be carried to the next life. In the next life, that person may exhibit neck pain or injury, thyroid malfunction, inability to wear turtleneck shirts, fear of or rage at authority, etc. That person, as a child, might feel unable to breathe when upset, reach for another's throat in a moment of anger, or find himself in repeated victim/tyrant situations. Until the initial trauma is identified and the glue is dissolved, variations of the experience will continue to repeat. And the little magnet shavings keep piling up until there's an overload.

Ongoing negative experiences, like in*toxic*ation due to use of medication or alcohol, going under general anesthesia, living in a dysfunctional environment, recurring abuse on any level, and prolonged exposure to extreme situations such as persecution or warfare, will increase the load or strain on the human energy field, intensifying the density, and encouraging it to manifest physically. I have described the lingering effects of an energetic density as similar to a bee stinger left in the skin. It continues to aggravate the organism long after the sting took place. If left in the skin, it might begin to fester and cause a systemic infection, and possibly death to the organism. As soon as the stinger is removed, the organism experiences relief and begins to heal. Traumatic densities can be removed with energy healing, and the organism can recover, even from past life traumatic events.

Once our human energy field is compromised, we become susceptible to invasion. Malfunctioning immunity can be an indication of pre-existing weakness in your energy field or karmic patterning. This is already commonly understood with regard to why we become susceptible to bacterial or viral infection. If we become run down for some reason – lack of sleep, lack of proper nourishment, exposure to extreme conditions or circumstances, we know we can fall ill. We simply need to extend that understanding to include invasion by foreign energies, such as the spirit of another person.

Spirit Possession

"On February 10th, 1907, the spirit of Mr. Thaw returned, and reiterated his statement that his son Harry was a psychic sensitive who was frequently subject to the influence of mischievous spirits. **He also urged upon humanity the great need for inquiry into the subject of spirit influence, saying that a proper understanding would prevent untold misery to both spirits and their unfortunate mortal victims."**

Dr. Carl Wickland, from <u>Thirty Years Among the Dead</u> 1930.

The young man referred to in the above passage had committed murder in 1906, while possessed by malevolent spirits. Dr. Wickland, quoted above, was a psychiatrist, and his wife was psychic. During a session, they were visited by Harry Thaw's father. This is what he said.

"I am Harry Thaw's father. Save my boy! Save my boy! He is not guilty. He is sensitive to spirit influence and has been all his life. He was always erratic and so excitable, we were afraid to correct him for fear he would become insane. But I see our mistake now. I did not understand the cause of Harry's queer actions while I was in the physical, but now, from the spirit side of life, I can see that Harry has been a tool in the hands of selfish, earthbound spirits most of his life. He was obsessed by revengeful spirits when he killed Stanford White."

Dr. Wickland discovered, when his wife went randomly into a trance one day and began to speak in another person's voice, that disembodied spirits could remain in the physical realm and cause the living significant harm. This caused the doctor to reconsider everything he had been taught about the causes of mental illness. With the help of his psychic wife, the doctor would meet with patients who were engaging in bizarre and self-destructive behavior, and see what was happening on the invisible side of those people's lives.

Dr. Wickland and his wife cured countless people who had been diagnosed as violently mentally ill. These people were destined to have frontal lobotomies and spend the rest of their lives in an institution. He and his wife held séances, and had dialogue with spirits that were attached to his patients. Mrs. Wickland must have seen Archangel Michael, just as my partner Patty had so many times, and realized He had a solution to the problem of recalcitrant spirits. Dr. Wickland tried to use reason and education to convince these spirits they had died decades before, and were harming someone else. If that failed, Archangel Michael and his helpers would come and take the attached spirit away. In our sessions, we took it one step further by offering compassion and empathy, and found that even the most intense anger and desire for revenge dissolved in the face of love. We called on Michael when that didn't work.

One of Dr. Wickland's patients was hospitalized because she had become a danger to herself. She kept punching herself in the face, cutting her hair and ripping off her own clothes. The spirit of an obnoxious man was attached to her. He refused to believe that he was dead and residing in her body. He was *sure* he was in his own body. He kept thinking someone was making him look like a girl, dressing him in skirts and wearing make up. It was embarrassing to him and he became furious. So he reacted violently, cutting his long hair, and trying to get these women's clothes and cosmetics off him. After this spirit was addressed directly, he left the patient and she recovered immediately. She was released from the mental hospital.

෪

While Dr. Wickland specialized in helping difficult spirits to the Light, Patty and I found ourselves clearing mainly lost and confused spirits. People with debilitating symptoms would be put in our path, and we would invite them to one of our sessions. We never started out to do this, mind you. At the beginning of my relationship with Patty, she was studying to be certified in Hypnotherapy. She had homework exercises requiring her to work with a partner. I happily volunteered. We started by simply sitting in meditation. As we sat, expressing our intention to bring about healing in a most appropriate way, images and situations would appear before us.

Patty had the visuals and the ability to determine the situation. I initially provided grounding so she could safely go into the deeper realms of consciousness, and eventually developed confidence in my own physical sensations and intuitive thoughts. When a thought seemed very prominent, or if I suddenly got a pain in my stomach or a stiff neck, I contributed that feedback. My feedback would verify or clarify something Patty was looking at, and helped us figure out what was happening. So, even though I wasn't visually psychic, I was extrapolating details in other ways.

Most sticky situations have fear at their root (I casually refer to the complex situation of spirit attachment as "stuck" spirits. It's based on my limited understanding of the magnetic nature of trauma). As our sessions evolved, my role expanded to that of ghost counselor. A person would come to us with an unresolved physical, mental or emotional problem, and Patty would "see" one or more spirits attached to the person. Patty would allow the stuck spirits to express words and emotions through her; I would offer dialog and reason, and together we offered compassion and resolution. The spirits would then feel safe to go to the Light, and would say goodbye. Moments later, our client would inform us that his or her symptoms were gone. After all these years, I have never lost the sense of exhilaration I feel after a successful de-possession.

When an unresolved emotional issue *wasn't* the cause of the ongoing attachment, we were dealing with a fragment of a person's energy. Ever heard that expression, scared stiff? When a person gets scared stiff, his psyche gets brittle, often fracturing, and a portion of his psyche remains in the time and space of the initial shock, while the rest of the person goes on to grow up, have relationships, etc. This fracturing can occur in the seconds before a person knows he is going to be killed, or harmed in a painful way. The intensity of witnessing or being a victim of extremely traumatic activity, violent death, sudden death, torture or abuse, or imposed unconsciousness, interrupts our usual program and causes us to malfunction. We "fracture" on an energetic level. Once there's a crack or a shattering of our protective energetic layering, we become susceptible to spirit attachment and other kinds of invasion which manifest as mental, emotional or physical disease. And a portion of our shattered self can remain with the perpetrator or witness. Sometimes we can witness unconsciously, or due to our own previous shattering, simply acquire a fragment of someone's shattered self by being in the wrong place at the wrong time. Sometimes the acquisition of another person's fragment happened in a past life and we have no recollection. All we have are symptoms that indicate something is wrong.

On occasion we had to go in, with focused intent, and retrieve fragmented portions of spirits or psyches, in order to bring about the health of our client. In those cases, the emotional component was no longer charged, but the shadow remained. While it was probably intense emotion that caused the initial fracturing, all that was left at this point was a shell. The presence of that shell would cast a shadow on some aspect of the host's existence, and cause some sort of phobia, disability or problem. Because the shell would not respond to our efforts at reason or emotional resolution, sometimes we had to call in the Angels to remove the shell and take it to its most appropriate place, so that our client would be free of a density that did not belong in his or her space.

☙

During our practice sessions for Patty's hypnotherapy homework, I was on the journey to recovering from my traumatic and extremely dysfunctional childhood. I was a single mom, desperately "hooked" on a depressive man who would not fulfill my needs, and my son was experiencing emotional extremes. I spent a lot of time crying for apparently no reason. My son seemed sad and estranged from his peers. His behavior had recently reverted to preverbal infantile fits. This was alarming to me because my son had been talking in complete sentences by the time he was 11 months old, and had always been known for his amazing ability to articulate. Now here he was, screaming and having tantrums when he was upset about something, seemingly unable to explain to me what was wrong. We were miserable. In fact, my six year old son had said he wanted to "go home and be with the Angels." That was the focus of our visit with Patty one day.

After guiding me through a relaxation exercise, Patty noticed a dark balloon-like energy floating behind my lower back. It had a cord that was attached to my second chakra area. There was also another cord that seemed to be going across the room, towards the door. My son, who was behind the door playing, suddenly went crazy, screaming and banging on the door. Patty quickly ascertained that the balloon-like object was the leftover energy of a baby I had lost in the first trimester of pregnancy, some years past. She was able to read the emotions of the baby energy that was still attached to me, and attached to my son. It didn't understand why it wasn't born into its own body. It was jealous of Sean, because he had a body, and it was trying to experience life vicariously through him. That explained my son's reverting to infantile emotions. And it was staying with me, partially from my own grief and guilt at the loss of the child. That explained my ongoing sadness and depression. The grief was unresolved because the baby energy was still with me, affecting me daily.

In afterthought, I realized how this was connected to my unhappy relationship. I had been very interested in marrying and having another child. My partner was decidedly not interested in doing either. I realized the baby was still trying to be born, and was influencing me, causing me to be obsessed with getting pregnant. In later sessions, further connections with that partner came to light.

By intent, Patty detached the cords from my son and me, and lovingly wrapped up the bundle. The cord connected to my son was very long and took a while to wrap up. Visually, she lovingly placed the bundle into a basket. Then she called on Angels and Beings of Light to come and help. She asked if there was a particular person from the other side who would like to come. We waited a minute, and she said, "Someone is coming." She began to describe a beautiful young man in such detail that I realized it was my sister's deceased first husband, who had died in a parachuting accident. Enno came out of the Light, took the bundle from Patty and went back into the Light.

Top, starting from right, Enno, my mom, one brother, me, and bottom, Enno.

It was perfect because we had all perceived Enno to be like a hero or champion when he was alive. He was an amazingly bright, handsome person, almost in an unreal way. He had been tall with blonde hair and blue eyes, a track star in high school and an expert marksman. He went into the Army after high school and was accepted into the 101st Airborne Paratroopers division. He was stationed at Eglin Air Force Base in Florida, where the 101st was practicing their jumps. He married my sister while on leave, and brought her back to Florida with him. His death was sudden, traumatic and violent, as the wind blew him and his parachute into a clump of tall trees that were concealing high-tension power lines. Before my sister's eyes, he was electrocuted, with a sickeningly loud electrical explosion sound and a blinding blue flash. He was killed instantly. His body tumbled out of the trees and floated eerily to the ground. My sister was nineteen years old then.

That event traumatized the whole family, as well as everyone who witnessed it. The entire base was closed for an investigation. Words cannot describe my range of emotions at the moment when my deceased, unborn-child was taken to heaven by the spirit of my brother-in-law who died when I was five. It was a relief in several respects, for in addition to knowing my unborn child was in the loving hands of a family member, I also now knew that Enno had gone to the Light, and that he too was okay. It was a profoundly healing experience for me, dissolving a trauma I had carried around my entire life, as well as healing my pregnancy-related grief.

When I thought the session would be ending, Patty informed me that my brother, who died in my childhood home in 1973, was also attached to me, influencing my moods, attitudes, appetites and desires. It was a very emotional encounter. She saw my brother in an athletic jacket, from the early 1960's, and his hair was slicked back in his favorite "ducktail" style. (See photo on page 90). It must have been a time in his life when he was relatively happy. Or perhaps my brother manifested that image because he knew I would recognize it.

Twenty years later, my brother and I were being given an opportunity to communicate for the first time since he died. I missed him terribly all of my life; it was an agonizing, desolate pain. It was a shadow of sadness I could never seem to shake. I turned at an early age to pain numbing substances like alcohol. Later, I named my only son after him - Sean. During the session, the spirit of my oldest brother told me that because we had been raised Catholic, he was sure he wouldn't be admitted into heaven after committing suicide, so he never even tried. He was afraid to be rejected. That, in itself, was tragically ironic because the main reason he killed himself was that people had been mean to him, and life had been cruel, and he only wanted to merge with the Oneness, where there was only Love. He took his life at the age of 22, after tearfully saying goodbye to our mother.

Full of doubt and still equipped with all of his depressive emotions and beliefs, my deceased brother hung around the earth plane, with me, and perhaps with my other siblings as well. After a time, my mother passed away. That made my brother even more reluctant to go, because he felt ashamed to face Mother. To him, it was worse than facing God. My mother had been absolutely devastated after his suicide. She was never the same again. Patty recognized the opportunity to allow him to end his painful limbo. Somehow she convinced him that he was right, there is only Love in the Light, and that he was welcome to go. She told him to look for someone in the Light, and my mother was there. They reunited, comforting each other, and he finally went into the Light, 20 years after his death.

I remember driving home from the session, laughing and crying as I realized he had been the source of my fascination with wearing a motorcycle jacket, among other things. After he left, my depression lifted and certain tendencies, mainly my interest in an unfulfilling relationship and self-destructive thoughts and feelings, vanished. My alcohol consumption dwindled to practically nothing, when it had been a constant struggle for almost two decades. Also, the symptoms my young son was having - extreme mood swings ranging from violent to suicidal depression - went away. Overall, our lives became much easier. And we were finally able to stop grieving.

ଓ

After several sessions with me being the client, we turned our attention to other folks. Actually, people were somehow put in my path. It happened everywhere I went. Perfect strangers would come up and start talking to me. They would begin describing symptoms or problems they were having, and if I got goose bumps, I knew they needed to be cleared. And so it went. I would arrange a meeting and the three of us would sit while Patty detected and removed densities. And the person's symptoms would vanish. We're talking paralysis, fibromyalgia, panic attacks and congestive heart failure, to name a few.

My partner's abilities included viewing a person's energy bodies and seeing dark spots or "dark snakelike things" as well as entities, spirits, etc. If she looked long enough at the dark spots, she would find herself in the midst of that person's past life experience, invariably a time when he died traumatically. The traumatic imprint is the dark spot in the energy field that is imbued with fear, and becomes a large obstacle in present time, being the foundation of phobias, strong aversions, supercharged emotions and physical disease.

When we were dealing with a spirit that was attached to someone and causing symptoms, Patty allowed the spirit to speak through her. Mostly, during sessions, we dealt with people who had mystery symptoms, and never dreamed that Aunt Martha could be attached to them. We counseled the spirit - bringing whatever was unresolved to conscious awareness and discussing it - satisfactorily resolving long-standing emotional conflict. Then we would guide it and any others to the Light, and our client's symptoms would dissipate.

It was very gratifying to be helping the spirits as well as the hosts. We developed a lot of compassion. Many spirits who don't cross over either believe they are wrongdoers and don't deserve to go to the Light, or have unresolved emotional issues - pain so real it transcends time and space. Sudden death or death while under anesthesia seem to confuse the spirits, and they go around trying to get information from people, not realizing they're dead, and get stuck in someone else's energy field. Sometimes it's a relative or a loved one who doesn't realize they're causing you harm, and they hang around trying to help you, to meet the baby or whatever your current life circumstances are, and you end up with all their symptoms.

We came to realize freeing them is doing a great service to the Collective Consciousness of humanity, and goes a long way towards creating world peace because it dissolves the fear-based patterning in which the discarnates are trapped. We were able to get spirits who thought they were worthless wrongdoers to help free thousands of other trapped spirits, and that made them feel redeemed. Then they would go into the

Light, feeling like they deserved to go. Thus a huge layer of patterning would be lifted. And that spirit would not have to repeat the victim/tyrant patterning the next time around. After each healing, there was a little less fear and a little more love, in the sea of Consciousness in which we all swim.

I would apply Reiki to the client before the session was over, to fill them up with Universal Life Force energy, to decrease the chances of their feeling a sense of grief, loss or emptiness after the spirit(s) left. The Reiki also decreased their chances of getting invaded again. Having a weak vibrational frequency is what makes people susceptible. We offered Reiki treatments and attunements, meditation lessons, and methods of self-care to keep the human energy field strong.

It's been most intriguing, satisfying work. I'm finding, being away from my psychic former partner, my intuitive skills are more highly developed than I thought, and I am able to help people, even by email. It was difficult to recognize my more subtle skills in the face of her obvious abilities. Patty always told me I *was* psychic, just in a different way than she is. I get intuitive hunches, and during sessions she always said that, at a crucial moment, I would say the perfect thing to begin the shift. I seemed to "know" what needed to be resolved and would pose just the right question or comment to the spirit, in order to bring the situation to a head, and allow healing to begin.

Patty has such rare and highly developed abilities, and I always felt I was groping in the dark until she verified something. In my mind, it was Patty who always brought the situation to resolution, even though she always validated my contribution, insisting it was an equal partnership. Because of our distance and my determination to keep going, I now go on instinct after viewing the results of the questionnaire I developed, and conducting an interview. I then instruct people how to free themselves of foreign energies. I am often able to help people who are plagued with seeing, feeling or hearing invisible things, or who may have unexplainable symptoms. People who have been under general anesthesia often come home with symptoms they didn't have when they went in for their surgery. I am interested in helping people free themselves from the hell of suffering from other people's symptoms.

I believe "spirit attachment" is as common as the common cold, and it is my intention to make spirit attachment a household phrase. It is my hope that this work will raise awareness about the invisible dangers of going under general anesthesia, drinking to blackout, experiencing or witnessing severe trauma, or knowing someone who has committed suicide. It is my educated opinion that people suffer from and perhaps even die of other people's symptoms all the time. They go to Doctors, who can't find causes, prescribe drugs, recommend surgery or refer them to psychiatrists. Many people just learn to live with their symptoms; even though they know what they're experiencing is not normal.

Regular folk can and should be fully informed how to clear their energy bodies after visiting such places as hospitals, convalescent homes, cemeteries, war zones, in order to maintain their health. Hospital personnel should also know the risks they face working in an area that is rife with discarnates, and be made aware of these simple, yet amazingly effective, methods by which to claim their space and clear themselves of foreign energies. One group who should not be without this Claim Your Space handbook is Paranormal Investigators. Anyone who works around the dead and dying should know the Claim Your Space routine by heart.

Whether one is dealing with an attached spirit or a traumatic density, the methods of clearing are basically the same. I wrote this book to demystify this process, give people the power to clear themselves and be well again. As Harry Thaw's father pointed out, there is much work to be done out there. I want people to realize they are not helpless. They can do their part to heal themselves and, at the same time, help stop the violence in the world by going inward and clearing their own personal trauma. That's what this book is about.

Pain in the Neck

When I first met Patty, I was suffering in an unfulfilling relationship. One of the physical problems I was suffering from at the time was a serious pain in the neck. I looked back about 15 years, remembering I'd had discomfort in my neck while in college, when I let my hair get long. The weight of it gave me a neck ache. Further back, I remembered I had plugged a hairpin into an outlet in the bathroom when I was about two years old. I still have the scars on my left hand. At some point, while in session, I remembered the current of that shock going in my hand, up my arm and ending with a *bam* in my neck. And beyond that, I remembered hearing my mother tell me that I had "sprung all her springs" by coming out shoulder first during my birth. The doctor told her she shouldn't try to have any more babies after that.

I determined that my neck pain was caused by a traumatic birth, and held in place partially by guilt that my being born had hurt my mother. During my mother's pregnancy with me, she had decided to leave my extremely abusive father. I am sure I absorbed her anxieties - feelings of fear about the future, distrust of "husband" and "father" and personal sense of worthlessness. What I would learn while working with Patty was that the traumatic imprint was already in my neck at the moment of my birth. It had started long before this lifetime.

I had tried chiropractic, acupuncture, stretching, prayer, and too many over-the-counter pain relievers, but nothing seemed to relieve the agony until we began doing the energetic clearing. In the course of several sessions, Patty kept finding lifetimes where I had been beheaded –a hapless villager during a raid by the Mongol hordes, etc. Because I was already several years into a Buddhist practice, I understood the implications of past life karma. Until that time, I thought the only way to eradicate the effects of negative karma was to chant Nam Myoho Renge Kyo and follow the Buddhist guidelines of monitoring my actions in thought, word and deed.

One of the beheading episodes involved the man with whom I was having a frustrating relationship in current time. He had been a samurai, and I, his daughter, in feudal Japan. He was loyal to the warlord, and I was caught planning a rebellion. He had to choose between the love of his daughter and loyalty to his warlord. He chose to behead his daughter (me). That corresponded with his current lifetime attraction, yet refusal to commit, to me, as well as neck pain and agonizing desire for him to love me fully. In session, we cleared the trauma of that lifetime, my neck improved, and that relationship began to fade away. And I moved closer to my goal of finding my perfect mate and creating a happy family. Incidentally that boyfriend, who was half Italian, half Swedish-American, told me that after the Vietnam War when he lived in Berkeley CA, he walked around the streets wearing a kimono robe and wooden Japanese sandals, and ate sushi all the time...

With each session, we reconciled some issue pertaining to neck trauma until we finally reached the one she perceived to be the first one, or the root cause. Interestingly, there was no linear timeline. The root cause was not in the "oldest" lifetime. Now we know that time is not linear, but that all of these lifetimes are probably happening parallel to each other.

In the "root cause" lifetime, I had been a Protestant nun, a devout and dedicated servant of God. But the Queen (Bloody Mary) was Catholic, and many Protestants were declared heretics and murdered by various means, including beheading. Right before the axe fell, Patty said I was enraged at God, feeling utterly betrayed, and I determined that I would NEVER again follow a spiritual path. In the midst of this session, my neck began to hurt terribly. The pressure was on. Since we were new at all this, we were trying to figure out how to proceed. Patty decided I should claim out loud that I was choosing a spiritual path no matter what, and forgive myself for allowing fear to take hold of me and believe that God had abandoned me. I claimed out loud that I was not going to fear my spiritual path, and the pain subsided.

I suddenly realized during the session, I had always HATED my first name. Everyone in my family called me by my middle name. And when some outsider came along and mistakenly called me by my first name, I would boil with rage, even at a very young age. I even went so far as to have it changed on my social security card as soon as I was old enough. Suddenly it all made sense. My first name was MARY.

More importantly, it was crucial for me to be firm in my conviction to follow my spiritual path without fear this time around. The trauma was aggravated because in the process of praying, meditating and chanting, the Light would come in through the top of my head, in an effort to go all the way through my body, as it should. But it was always stopped by that density in my neck, the traumatic imprint of the physical damage that was held in place by my sworn oath NEVER to be spiritual again. She said when I chose the spiritual path this time around, the neck problems and pain reared up. The more I sat in meditation, the worse it got, until we were able to clear it. I am glad I never succumbed to the pressure of having surgery, and I feel sure the energetic clearing is what finally freed me from the stranglehold of pain and physical limitation. I realized nothing is permanent, and that by dealing with the problem on the energetic level, I was able to put an end to the physical symptoms.

Without a psychic, you can take steps to protect yourself and remove densities you believe you may have. If you wish to be free of limiting and painful symptoms, then the procedures outlined in this book can help you free yourself from these invisible but debilitating obstacles. Whether you suddenly feel ill, or if you have been ill a long time without cure, you have choices. If you have a fever or other indicator of bacterial infection, you should go to the doctor. But no matter what changes you experience, it can't hurt to spend a few minutes taking these preventive measures that may make your symptoms vanish as quickly as they arrived.

In the Spin – and Out Again

As I said, a family's energy probably already matches the energies of a haunted house, in order to be pulled into it. My parents had been living in a whirlwind, of violence, oppression, death and world war, for several years before they happened upon the house. Their psyches were surely fractured from witnessing massive human suffering, people killing people and other wartime atrocities. They must have been in shreds after World War II. And before that, there was surely pain from early childhood abandonment, since both had been abandoned by one or both parents at a very early age. They each had layer upon layer of relatively fresh trauma energy heaped on them, and had, inadvertently, attracted the house experience to them. There was probably something familiar about the feeling in the house when they first walked through it.

This is not to say every person who survived World War II ended up living in a haunted house. Each person, based on experience, develops a 'spin.' Someone else's spin, based on a different cultural and experiential set up, would put them in a different situation. If you're a rare person, there may be no evidence of trauma in your life, and therefore no illness or scarcity or issues of abandonment. But usually people have some kind of spin that manifests as domestic violence or child abuse, alcoholism or drug abuse, phobias, dysfunctional relationships or physical illness. Whatever the situation, it needs to be cleared to prevent long-term illness and debilitation.

ଓ

In the Spin

For the 30 years my family lived in the haunted house, you could hear creaking floor boards, see shadowy things, feel like you were trapped in certain rooms, and experience sheer terror just walking around in many areas of the house. I believe it was haunted by multiple spirits, some of whom had been victims of betrayal and violent death, hapless victims of persecution and abuse. Others were alcoholic and otherwise "dark" people, not nice people in life, who didn't go to the Light when they died. You can't have just one side of any equation. Where there are victims, you will also find tyrants. People tend to relate to or understand the victim energy, but when they encounter the tyrant energy, they tend to believe it is evil. In the midst of a terrible act, the perpetrator can be as traumatized as the victim. They were all still there, caught in the spin of trauma.

One of the most haunted rooms was upstairs, at the top of the back stairs. Just getting to it was hair-raising. Off the kitchen, next to a tiny pantry, was a set of steep, narrow, winding stairs that led up to this room. Anyone with claustrophobia would never have been able to get up those stairs. The stair well was imbued with fear. The room at the top of the stairs got inherited by the oldest child, each in succession. It was on the outskirts of the core of the house and there was an easy exit down the stairs and out the kitchen door, so I guess my parents felt you had to be older to be alone in there.

My oldest brother was second to go in, after my sister. In his late teen years, he decided to make it a black light room, painting all the walls black and the ceiling purple. He and his friends would stay in there for hours and hours, and drink and do drugs. I think many people were experimenting with drugs in the early and mid sixties, but I feel our family and friends were all heavily influenced by entities who wanted to vicariously enjoy the darker side of human pleasures through them. My brother felt compelled to shoot himself in the stomach with a .22 caliber rifle while in the room. I have no idea why he shot himself, but he must have thought it was a reasonable solution to his problems. He didn't die at that time. My mother said, starting at the age of 16, my brother tried to kill himself at least once a year, until at age 22, he finally succeeded. All those years, the room at the top of the stairs had been his bedroom.

His heroin addiction developed while he stayed in that room. My mother said the addiction was the result of his being treated for the gunshot injury, and the sudden end of his morphine prescription upon release from the hospital. While there are always other explanations for our choices and actions, looking back, I feel sure our thoughts, feelings and actions were all influenced by invisible forces in that area of the house.

One vivid memory is the story of two men, strangers to my mother, who went up the back stairs to see Sean in the creepy bedroom. He had successfully undergone rehabilitation once, but still had a reputation for being involved in drugs. He said, even though for weeks prior to their arrival, he had resisted the demands of these strangers to find drugs for them, they persisted until he relented, just to get them to leave him alone. The day they came in and headed up the stairs, my mother was filled with a sense of dread. A few moments later, my brother was led down the stairs in handcuffs. It was yet another classic set up, a case of entrapment, similar once again to the Kelsey incident. One man had led authorities to my brother in order to reduce his own sentence, and they pressured my brother to find drugs for them. This incident resulted in my brother being sent to prison for two years.

I think nearly everyone in the family had bad experiences in that particular room. When another brother inherited the room, he slept with an iron bar under his mattress, because he always felt there were intruders, and he needed to be ready. He would wake up in the middle of the night, sure he'd heard something, and go running out in the hall, brandishing his iron pipe, but there'd be nothing there. He lived in a constant state of paranoia and anxiety while that was his bedroom. His tenure in the room at the top of the stairs also included heavy alcohol and drug use. In hindsight, it seems obvious to me we had all fallen into some pre-existing pattern of depraved behavior. It's surprising nobody had considered this while we lived there, but we were all so busy trying to recover from the latest crisis, we didn't have time to analyze.

Once, in broad daylight, my mother and I actually felt trapped in that bedroom. I was cleaning the room, and I could hear noises as if people were moving around, but it was in the walls, where there really was no place to *be*. My heart started pounding so loud it was deafening me. There was an overwhelmingly menacing feeling. I was afraid "it" could hear me breathing. It's hard to control your breath when your heart is beating like mad. Rather than run out, I called in my mother, and she heard the noises and creaks too. We looked at each other like two deer in the headlights. Her idea was to quietly tiptoe out the door and bring the telephone into the room with us! The phone was on a really long cord. It was all at once desperate and absurd.

Logically, if someone were in the house and trying to "get" us, all they had to do was cut the cord, and we'd be trapped. It's funny now, because I realize we could simply have walked downstairs and outside. But at the time, we were absolutely paralyzed with terror. We felt sure some menacing force knew we were in the room and would do us harm if we spoke out loud or behaved in normal ways. We were trapped in the Vortex of Hell. I can't help but wonder if someone, a long time ago, was being pursued by people who were coming up the stairs, and that person truly could not get out of the room. That person truly was trapped. I wouldn't be surprised if that person was shot in that room, as well. And all the energy of the incident was still there, affecting us in the 1970's.

The bathroom was right next to that room, and it was also very creepy. There were two doors leading to the bathroom. When I was little I was afraid to flush the toilet because I knew "something" would realize I was in there and come and "get" me. The feeling was very similar to my Indian fantasy in later years, and the feeling I had while alone in my bedroom. After a while, my mom and sister refused to accompany me anymore. It was always a tough decision to decide which door was safer to exit, because I knew I "it" would get me if I chose the wrong door. I would often sneak out quietly, in order to escape safely, only to have my sister demand, "Did you flush? Go back and flush!" It was ongoing terror...

For some unknown reason, I decided to electrocute myself in there when I was two years old, and take a whole bottle of baby aspirin when I was three. Both of those incidents could have killed me, but didn't. And when I was about four, I tripped and fell in the hallway leading from the bathroom to the main part of the upstairs, and hit my forehead on a sharp object, splitting open the skin on my forehead. Three potentially fatal accidents happened to me within three years in one small area of the house. In the same hallway several years later, my mother slipped on a rug and fell flat on her back. She lost her breath and I was terrified, thinking she had perhaps broken her back and would be paralyzed. Luckily, she sustained no permanent damage from that fall. But the feeling of terror, even pending death, was ever present.

After living in the haunted bedroom for several years, my oldest brother took a fatal dose of Methodone in the creepy bathroom. He died later that night in 1973, downstairs in the living room. The two of us overdosed in the bathroom, exactly ten years apart. What would possess an innocent little child to explore a bathroom she was normally terrified to be alone in, climb up onto the sink, open the medicine cabinet, and consume an entire bottle of baby aspirin? What would possess a young man to be absolutely convinced taking his life was the *only* way out of his current predicament? Was it *really* as bad as he thought? Or was he being influenced by someone else's feelings? Were we caught in the magnetic pull of past traumatic experience, repeating itself like a skip in a record?

While many of these details can be explained away with other reasons, I am always suspicious when such blatant patterning presents itself. While my brother's course of events could have had a variety of explanations, it still smacks of perverted spirit influence, or the magnetic pull of pre-existing trauma. I can't help feeling certain our thoughts, emotions and decisions were influenced while we were living in that house.

My sister shared one memory with me, of 'something coming over' my father. He once got a glazed look in his eye and then began to assault my oldest brother, who was only a child at the time. The kids had been playing out on the back porch, at the base of the stairwell leading to the creepy upstairs bedroom. They didn't know what they had done to annoy my dad. He picked up my brother and began to slam him into the wall, over and over again. My sister thought our brother was going to be killed, so she (also a child) took a broom and struck my father in the back with it, at the risk of drawing my father's wrath upon her, so he would leave my brother alone. She said he stopped, put down my brother, and turned around. Recognition returned to his eyes, and they waited with bated breath for the next part of the punishment, but he walked away as if nothing had happened.

I think my father was possessed intermittently. He was psychically sensitive, referring to himself as a moonchild, because he was born under the sign of Cancer, and Cancerians tend to be psychic. He did unspeakable things to his wife and children in the house in the fourteen years before my birth. I know my father used hypnosis on family members... I can't go into too much detail here, but suffice it to say, by the time I was born my mother and all four siblings were deeply traumatized.

Because of the path my own healing took, I realized the house was extremely haunted, and we were all victims. During one psychic session, the focus was on the youngest brother in our family, who was 'frozen' on the basement landing. In her mind, Patty saw him as 6 to 8 years old, wearing a bathing suit. He had been frightened so badly, a part of his psyche had fractured, and was still there, standing in stark terror at the top of the basement stairs. I told her my father had rigged the light switch with a tape recorder so the light wouldn't come on, but monster noises would play. The older boys knew about it, and probably had tricked the youngest to go in, and they flipped the switch and slammed the door, leaving him alone in the dark, with the musty smell and scary noises coming up the steep flight of stairs from pitch black basement. At the time of that remote healing, we cleared the whole house with our unique method of prayer and intention. It was in about 2000, and my brother was 46 years old.

The indication we had, of violent or perverted predecessor energy in the basement, was the super creepy, panic-producing feeling down there. It was a field stone foundation with a dirt floor. The earth smelled ancient. When I told the psychic every dog we ever owned dug furiously behind the basement stairs, she suddenly screamed. She said she could see a very malevolent man had been murdered and buried under the stairs. She said he looked like some kind of pirate or smuggler. His spirit never left the house.

She said, "Oh yeah, he used to LOVE to give your father ideas on how to torment the children."

Clearly, my father was a sick man, whether from genetics, early childhood abandonment, doing spy stuff in World War 2, or all of the above. He was severely damaged, perverted and abusive. Still, the question that always comes to me is, why would a man do such things to his own children? The answer I have come up with is, some of the time, it wasn't him. My siblings will probably disagree with me, but I feel whoever was doing the more severely abusive and sick things to my mother and us, temporarily possessed my father. Whoever it was didn't love us or care about us in the least. We were objects of someone else's seriously deranged perversions. I believe, in the case of a house thick with accumulated energies, one's weaknesses become significantly amplified. Add alcohol to the mix, and you have disaster. What an unfortunate combination. What a nightmare for us...

In spite of all the horrifying activity, ironically, my mother developed a powerful obsession for the house. Magnetic pull? Every bit of energy she had was involved in keeping the house at all costs, right up until her death. She acted as if the family would absolutely perish if we were to lose it. That was extremely ironic, since we so often felt like we would perish due to weird occurrences in the house, and my brother actually died in the house. I know we had financial difficulty, but it's strange I never once heard her consider living anywhere else. It would have been much better for all of us if we had moved out sooner, but she was stuck like glue... she never figured out how to get out of the undertow, to swim out the side. Mom died at the age of 62, while we still resided in the house.

After Mother died, the feeling of keeping the house at all costs suddenly transferred to one of my siblings. In spite of clear directions to me in her Last Will and Testament to sell the house and divide the proceeds, that particular sibling said he would fight me every step of the way. There was no reasoning with him. At the time I didn't recognize the patterning. Now I can't help wondering if one of the many possessing entities in the house was one of the original owners, who couldn't bear to part with the house he built with his own two hands... Perhaps he had first possessed my mother, and then my brother after she passed away. It is one possible explanation for their seemingly irrational attachment to the house.

And Out Again

The work of helping people clear themselves of foreign energies is a personal vocation for me. I can't think of anything else I'd rather do at this point. People are so often caught up in the spin of this or that drama, they don't realize they still have the ability to stop the ride and control their destiny. Usually people don't think about clearing themselves of inner magnets of victim energy, for instance, until they are in desperate trouble or battling a life threatening affliction.

☙

At this stage of my life, I don't wait for things to become desperate before I claim my space. If my neck flares up after a particularly stressful week or an uncomfortable encounter, I immediately claim my space. I know other people's negative emotions are a form of "foreign" energy I do not have to accept in my energy field. People are so conditioned to believe certain pains or physical problems will NOT go away without a doctor or, in my case, a chiropractor's help. But I have challenged my own beliefs in this area. When my neck used to go out, I'd panic and call the chiropractor. I spent thousands of dollars when my family couldn't really spare the money.

One Sunday we had to go to a party and my neck was suddenly very stiff and sore. The pain made me absolutely miserable. Even though I couldn't think of how it might have been caused, I felt sure my neck was "out" and I would have no relief until I was able to get to the Chiropractor later in the week. When we arrived at the party, my husband had to help me get out of the car, and I could not turn my head at all. It caused nausea and spasms in my shoulders and down my back. We met a psychic healer on the way into the party and, seeing the level of my distress, he offered to give me a session on the spot. His impression was, someone who was angry at me had "thrown" negative energy at me. He silently worked on my neck for a minute or two, when I suddenly realized all my pain was *gone*. If I hadn't already been a believer, that episode would have done the trick. So now, when I feel like my neck is out, I don't pick up the phone first. I say my prayers first. I claim my space and ask my guardian angels and healing angels to take my pain away so I can get up and go to work in the morning. I know my intention can shift everything in my life.

According to the Law of Attraction, we create our own reality, and I find it to be true. Some people think about the concept on a grand scale, but when they get a head cold, they call the doctor and go get pills! They don't even think about intending to be well. I have learned to apply the concepts of self-healing to nearly every event in daily life. If my daughter hurts herself for no apparent reason, if one of us has a headache, we do the Claim Your Space exercise. If I am noticing people in my environment are reacting negatively to me, I claim my space. If I am fearful or panicky for some reason, I claim my space. If I have the feeling something bad is going to happen, I claim my space. I now realize many things occur on the energetic level long before they ever show up in the physical. I listen to my emotions.

Karma is action in thought word and deed. Your thoughts, words and deeds generate your karma. But your feelings usually determine what you are thinking, saying and doing. Emotionally charged words and deeds usually produce some sort of karmic effect. They also produce traumatic events that can stick in your energy field for lifetimes. So, if you can monitor your emotions, you can learn to clear issues up long before they become crises. Keeping your emotional body free of obstacles will keep you happy and healthy for years to come. One easy and effective way to keep your emotional body free of obstructions is to claim your space.

One healthy side effect of regularly practicing claiming your space is you get to know yourself. You are, in essence, learning to manage your energy bodies. Paying attention to your life on the subtle levels enables you to learn to live in the "flow." It's listening to your "inner voice." It's recognizing the Divine within you. When you can do that, you will naturally recognize the Divine in everyone and everything else. Everyone carries some sort of patterning, some weakness, some trauma. And those items obstruct the flow of Divine light into your human energy field. There's always a story, or many stories, attached to it. You can spend decades trying to trace them to their source, like I did, or you can simply assume if you're having some kind of problem in your life, there is a root cause somewhere in your energy bodies. You can begin to dissolve the obstacles by claiming your space, kicking out energies that were placed in you - by traumatic experience, early childhood conditioning, or what have you - and finding a spiritual practice of some kind, so you can fill yourself up with Light. When the dense obstacles have been dissolved from your being, you are free to fill up your consciousness with love, abundance, prosperity, devotion, good health, all the things that make you feel truly alive. You can begin to feel whole. As Jennifer Berezan says in the opening lines of her song on the album, Returning to the Mother of Us All, "I am Holy, I am Whole." Why not work on retrieving all of your fractured pieces and keeping your space clear, so you don't get sucked into a vortex of a hell of your own making? Whatever you're putting out, you're going to get in return. So, why not get your vibrational frequency humming a happy tune, and attract the same to yourself in daily life? This book can show you how to free yourself of debilitating inner magnets.

My mother's Aunt, right, and colleagues

Healing and Religion

My father dabbled in something, I'm not sure what. I often wondered if he learned some sort of mind control during spy training with the OSS in World War II. The four kids who were born before me went through Hell. When my parents died, I found a card with my Dad's handwriting on it. It was a hypnosis schpeil, *"You're getting very sleepy,"* and I felt he had used it on my mother or siblings in order to manipulate them. It was deeply ironic, in that my mother had come from a devout Catholic family. In my house, it was truly an ongoing battle between good and evil. And he had the upper hand for many reasons – my mother was pregnant much of the time, running around after little ones, sleep deprived. Plus he was more than twice her size, with a frightening temper. And as my mother always said, "he was very persuasive." He was large and in charge.

My mother referred to their 15-year marriage as the Reign of Terror. When I was born, I was the fifth child, she was 41, and all the others were either teens or almost teens. After enduring what must have seemed like an eternity of hellish experiences, and despite the strong Catholic imprinting that a good wife never divorces her husband, she had decided during her pregnancy with me, she would leave him, no matter what. She told me she had decided it would be utterly wrong to bring another child into that situation. I suppose she could have chosen to terminate the pregnancy, but she was determined to have me. She convinced my father to leave her and the children in the house before I was born, and he went off to do other things. It must have been a daunting thing to do with winter coming and a baby on the way. I was born in November. There were unpaid bills, taxes, the need for heating oil and utilities, clothing and food for a pregnant woman and four children. It was stressful and probably frightening, but without a doubt, it was much better than living with him. Now, they felt free of the tyrant. They thought all their troubles would leave with him.

I grew up feeling surrounded by war-torn survivors. Shell-shocked and shattered, they were. I don't know how many of those terrible events might have taken place had we not been living in one of the oldest and most haunted houses on the Eastern Seaboard (my opinion), but I think any character weakness my parents, siblings and I may have had, was accentuated a thousand fold because we were being influenced by unsettled spirits and layers of traumatic energy in the house. After my father left, the evidence of haunting was before us daily.

With him gone, the spirits had only us to mess with. I can just imagine the spirits of deranged people thinking, "What fun - severely abused, vulnerable teenagers, like puppets on a string. Let's give them the urge to drown their sorrows in drink, and see what wicked things we can make them do to themselves and each other."

☙

After my brother's suicide when I was eleven, I began reading metaphysical books and seeking information about the true nature of existence, what lies beyond "the veil" and how we are all connected forever. I really NEEDED to know what my mother had told me was true. When we were in complete anguish over the loss of my oldest brother, she said he was still with us, he hadn't really gone anywhere. My eleven-year-old mind wondered, "How come I can't SEE him or TOUCH him?" It was pure agony. Little did we know at the time, her statement was truer than any of us had realized. Later, both my father and mother passed away over an 18-month period, during my years at community college. By the time I was 20, I had no parents, we were required to sell the house, and the surviving siblings were scattered in every way. I was lost.

In the midst of losing everything familiar to me - wondering what I, an unloved and unwanted twenty year old with no direction, was supposed to do on the planet - I spent a great deal of time and money trying to blot it all out with alcohol and social distractions. One of my best friends had become a bartender in a local tavern and I often visited her. Somewhere in the blur, I met the man who would become my first husband. It had become clear within a few months of life with my English husband that circumstances with him were much more unstable and frightening than I had become accustomed to in the Vortex of Hell. I stayed on the alcoholic roller coaster with him for a few years, until I became pregnant with my first child. When I was suddenly incapable of holding down a beer, and no longer confused about what was right and what was wrong, I knew times were about to change.

I still say my son came into this world to save my life. It seems becoming pregnant had snapped me out of deep denial of my circumstances. During that pregnancy, I allowed myself to *feel* again. I took good care of myself and tried to be calm for the baby. That alone was a significant challenge, considering the high levels of dysfunction, fear, anger, betrayal and violence in which I was living. I felt so alone. I found myself missing my mother a great deal, wishing I could go home. Knowing there was no home to which to return plummeted me into the depths of despair, and was probably why I stayed in the relationship much longer than I should have. I was desperate. I prayed for guidance and searched my soul for answers that would lead me to the correct path, because up to that point I most certainly had NOT been on it. At the time, I couldn't tell it was all an extension of my childhood patterning. I was caught in a spin much larger than myself.

Over a four-year period, three miraculous things happened to me. First, before I left my marital home in Connecticut, but after it was clear I must in order to save myself, I received a phone call from an old high school friend. We had fallen out of touch and I was surprised to hear from her. She asked how things were going and I opened up like an avalanche. I told her I couldn't tolerate the situation any longer. She invited me to come and stay with her in northern California. Because her voice of reason felt like the only life raft available in a vast sea of uncertainty, I pulled up stakes and left. I realized a few weeks into my new life in Arcata, CA, I was pregnant. Even though going back to my husband was crazy, it seemed better than going through pregnancy amongst long lost friends and strangers in a strange town. So after about six weeks, I decided to return to Connecticut.

Right before I left CA, my friend and I were walking when she asked, "Didn't you ever wonder why I called out of the blue to ask how you were?"

I guess I hadn't.

She said, "I wasn't going to tell you, but I think I should, since you've decided to go back."

What she said next dramatically defined the direction of my future.

She said, "Your mother came and visited me one night. She was standing at the foot of my bed. She told me you were in trouble, and asked if I could help you."

That was somewhat astonishing, considering my mother had died 5 years before; but not too astonishing, because I knew my friend had experienced astral projection in her teen years, and I had always believed love transcended time and space. In my blindness I had been treading in very dangerous waters, and my mother came back from the dead to warn me to get out - miracle material, as far as I'm concerned.

The next miracle was my introduction to Buddhism while my son was an infant. I still have the journal where I had written I was seeking the right spiritual practice. I was back with my husband at the time, albeit temporarily. I was introduced to the wondrous spiritual practice by Tina Turner's autobiography, "I, Tina." Ironically, I only read it because my husband was a big fan of hers. She traveled in British musicians' circles, and so did he. In the book, she explained how the Buddhist practice had protected her from her violent, drug addicted husband, allowed her to challenge her karma and make all her dreams come true. I wanted that. I found the strength to leave him.

Once I began to practice Nichiren Buddhism, I was able to manifest my own miracles almost daily. People came out of the woodwork to help the baby and me, offering airfare from the east coast to the west, a place to stay, all kinds of material necessities. I managed to manifest an apartment I could afford, a return to school, a car, a job and really good friends. I was able to come back to life. But there was still a lingering depression and a sense of loss, of separation from family.

For the two years I had been in California and away from the east coast, I had constantly felt bereft and had been praying to meet someone who would feel like family. After chanting like that for a while, I met the woman who would shed light on what had been at the root of my suffering, and actually take steps to REMOVE the imprinting from my energy field. Patty French was my third miracle. Patty was the same astrological sign as my mother, and possessed what seemed like feelings of unconditional love toward me, for some unknown reason. Our relationship held so much, I couldn't have possibly imagined at the time how the next fourteen years would unfold.

༺ઝ༻

One of the most wonderful things I realized was time is not linear. Everything is happening at once. Even though we say "past life" there really is no such thing. I believe we are multidimensional beings, and have many lifetimes happening concurrently. Phobias and afflictions, whose roots cannot be traced to any event in the current, conscious lifetime, can be attributed to an event happening in one of our parallel lifetimes. Luckily, on some level, we learn from events and mistakes in all of our existences. And we also accumulate karma - benefits and consequences - based on all the thoughts, words and deeds we express in all the lifetimes.

That's why energy healing works so well, because it goes straight to the problem and begins to dissolve it. Whether it started in my childhood or in a previous life is now immaterial. If I wish it healed, it is. That's the way Buddhism works, too. Based on the belief that time is not linear, I took comfort in the idea that my spiritual seeking, soul searching and efforts in healing were benefiting all members of my family, whether they were dead or alive.

I have been fortunate to learn two methods that enable people to heal themselves relatively instantly, Buddhism, chanting Nam Myoho Renge Kyo to eliminate negative karma and create good fortune, and Energy Healing in the forms of psychic clearing and Reiki. It is probable other forms of prayer are also effective, but I have not personally experienced such dramatic results by other means. I have come to believe with these two vehicles and the realization that time is not linear, most emotional and mental traumas can be eliminated, as if they never happened. I mean - even tumors, the emotional effects of traumatic experience, illnesses that don't seem to go away, severe aches and pains, lifelong depression - things that leave people debilitated, can be completely cured, and quickly.

There is a new body of evidence developing in the area of DNA research supporting this theory (See KRYON book 12, by Lee Carroll). With the advent of the movies, <u>What the Bleep Do We Know</u>? and <u>The Secret</u>, it is mainstream information that we are constantly manifesting our own reality moment to moment with our choices. While those wonderful bits of information might not explain why we sustain early childhood abuse, they do offer the knowledge that we can change things NOW. Buddhism offers an explanation about why we experience traumas in early childhood; it is karmic retribution, or the natural and logical consequences of our own actions, for something that took place in one of our other existences.

That's a very long way of saying, I firmly believe that most of what has been done can be undone, and associated symptoms can vanish in the healing process. I was getting closer to understanding what my mother had said all those years ago when my brother died. There is no separation. We really are all One, all the time. I have learned your FEELINGS are your biggest clues to healing. If you ignore them, the rage, resentment and betrayal stay bottled up and eventually manifest in your body as physical and mental disease.

I understand many people avoid meditation and therapy for fear of reliving painful memories, but inward is the only place to go. I believe in the protection of Light Beings, Guardian Angles and Healing Angels. And I believe, like when I was dealing with an abusive husband, if you continue to fear the problem, it gains more power over you. Many people told me that while I was in the depths of the abuse. I challenged him argumentatively, even though I was afraid, and I was beaten many times, and I truly thought he would kill me if I stood up to him fully. But when I finally did, the opposite happened. The whole thing popped like a bubble, and I was suddenly out of it. I was out of the undertow, and I didn't drown.

I left with my infant child, determined to find a spiritual practice and pull myself together. As soon as I made the decision, I was supported every step of the way. It was like magic. The path before me was unknown and I had no resources whatsoever, but I was handed everything I needed. I discovered the joy of manifesting rather than reacting to my reality. The terrible spell I had been under was broken by my intention to create a better life for my young child, and I was breathing fresh air for the first time in my life. All it took was a heartfelt decision and belief in the support of the invisible realms. I think most folks call that faith.

ങ

Buddhism had a lot to do with my learning how to manifest, and how to accept responsibility for EVERYTHING in my life, even the things that happened when I was too little to understand. I was advised to develop compassion for the ones I'd rather blame for all my suffering. It's not easy to pray for the happiness of someone who left scars on your face and in your heart. I had become accustomed to sitting at home with no food and no money while my husband was out cavorting with friends. He'd be gone for days at a time, and then show up one day and rifle through all the coat pockets in the closet, looking for money. With his two dollar treasure in hand, he'd leave again with hardly a word in my direction. I would sit in the living room, clutching the baby, wondering what would become of us, and when I would see him again. It was always a mixed feeling. I needed a partner in the marriage, but having him home usually wasn't very safe. It dawned on me one freezing cold day when the cupboards were empty and there had been no heat for some time, that he had truly abandoned us. I mean, it wasn't just emotional abandonment, it was physical, real. With that thought crystallized in my mind, instead of just sitting there like a helpless victim waiting for him to come home, I began to take steps to save my son and me.

Even though it was hard, several months later when we were out, I chanted for my ex-husband's happiness twice a day, until eventually I really meant it. I knew it was impossible to engage in dialogue with him without arguing, but I learned dialogue wasn't necessary for resolution of the situation. I accepted spiritual responsibility for everything that had happened between us, and expressed appreciation to his higher self for giving me a learning experience. And when I truly did have appreciation for him one day, he called out of the blue and announced he wished to begin making child support payments. That's a story in itself, and is an example of what the Buddhists call 'actual proof' of the effectiveness of the practice.

When my son Sean was 17 months old, we went to a Buddhist temple. On that day, it was official, we were Buddhist and it was against our religion to kill anything, especially a human being. I practiced chanting and praying twice a day while he was very young. We had weekly meetings at our apartment, and the sound of chanting pleasantly pervaded my living environment. When I met my second husband, he began chanting too.

Buddhism teaches you to take responsibility for everything that happens to you, and gives you the tools to "change poison into medicine." By chanting the phrase Nam Myoho Renge Kyo, (Devotion to the Mystic Law of the Simultaneity of Cause and Effect), you can eliminate personal suffering, arouse the protective forces of the Universe, and accumulate good fortune and benefit for yourself and your family, 7 generations back and 7 generations ahead. Since my family had been through hell with my father, and I with my husband, I had a lot to chant about. In addition to manifesting an apartment, a car, a job, an opportunity to go back to College, I asked for and found a peace-loving, sober husband who would be a good father for Sean.

Around 1996, my best friend and psychic co-worker, Patty, invited me to sit with an "Enlightened Teacher". Leslie Temple-Thurston of Corelight taught us about our many 'subtle' or 'light' bodies, chakras, multidimensional existence, etc. We would sit with her four to eight hours a month, and she would guide us through intense meditations. I completed her Spiritual Warrior training program.

For a long while, I was conflicted in my beliefs because the Buddhists are non-Theistic. They do not believe in God per se, but in the True Entity of All Phenomena as life itself, Dependent Origination - all beings are connected - and the Law of the Simultaneity of Cause and Effect. But my Enlightened Teacher said there is a higher law than the Law of Cause and Effect, and that is the Law of Grace. She said if you ask God (or Spirit or Source) for help, karma and trauma can be lifted from you. That's where I began to have serious questions. I allowed my flow to be interrupted by this semantic and illusory problem for a long time. I tend now to believe it is all the same, understanding that trauma and karma are lifted from me due to my own intent and efforts, not because an external source bestowed a blessing on me.

While I was practicing Buddhism, I realized I also love Jesus. I believe Jesus was an Enlightened Master who went East, was exposed to Buddhist and Hindu philosophies, and brought them back to Israel. It was those very Buddhist teachings - of compassion and mercy, the Golden Rule, cause and effect - that made him so different from the Jews, and got him into so much trouble. But it was the next appropriate step.

My Enlightened Teacher said, before Jesus, people were unable to hold any Divine light in their bodies. That's why the priests were so powerful as intermediaries between people and God. It is said the Ark of the Covenant contained the souls of all the people of the 12 tribes of Israel. If anyone but the appointed priest or King (King David?) came near it, they would be electrocuted through its sheer electromagnetic force.

Jesus came to teach us how to open our hearts and our crown chakras, so we could receive divine light into our bodies. We had to have our hearts broken, wrenched in two, by his torture and crucifixion, so we could begin to receive Light directly into our bodies. It was an initiation for Humanity. We could be 'like him.' We could forgive, heal, love unconditionally, and be one with God. Formerly, all those things were solely in the domain of the priests. That's one of the reasons the Jewish priesthood perceived Jesus as such a threat. They would be out of a job if everyone believed the messages of Jesus. He was eliminating middle management. In 2005, I wrote an article about this subject.

Bringing in the Light

From the standpoint of bringing in the Light, what is the significance of the birth of Jesus and his subsequent crucifixion? The placement of his injuries, the "crown" of thorns, the fact that he was put on a cross? How do you think he might have explained getting Christ Consciousness into us if he were here today? Why do all images of Jesus and Saints show an aura around their heads? What is the meaning of the story in Matthew about the bridesmaids keeping their lamps lit? (Matthew 25: 1-14) Are we the lamps? If so, how do we stay lit?

If you think of the whole Jesus experience as an initiation for Mankind to begin holding his own Light, all the details of Christ's message, torture and death have significance. Why did Jesus sustain injuries in his hands and feet? Why was there a "crown" of thorns? I believe these places were made the focus of pain in order to bring people's attention to them. There are chakras, or energy portals, in the hands and feet, as well as along the core. The hand and feet chakras needed to be consciously opened in order to facilitate the flow of Light through the body. And the "crown" brought attention to the crown chakra, the opening at the top of the head, where God gets in.

One of my teachers, Leslie Temple-Thurston of Corelight, said in order to have your heart (chakra) permanently opened, it sometimes requires a heartbreaking, painful event. In the words of Carly Simon from her song called Coming Around Again, "Don't mind if I fall apart, there's more room in a broken heart." The torture and crucifixion of Jesus was so brutal and profound, it has broken the hearts of millions of compassionate people for two thousand years. From the standpoint of needing to open the heart chakras and activate the Light bodies of all Mankind, every aspect of that terrible event was necessary and productive.

More recently we had similar events I believe were further initiations for Mankind to be more open-hearted, and hold even more Light in our bodies than ever before. In 1997, the world lost two "angels on earth" within two months of each other – Lady Diana and Mother Theresa. Millions of people were absolutely devastated - broken hearted - over the deaths of those incredible human beings. When we expressed concern to our teacher, "What will become of the world now that these pillars of Light have left the planet," she explained the energy hasn't gone anywhere. It is now up to each person to hold more of that energy. Now, more than ever, each person is being prompted by Spirit to hold more Light. This is how we will make the quantum leap from a world of fear and war to one of love and everlasting peace.

Jesus' message of unconditional love and mercy was for all people, regardless of their gender or socio-economic standing. He was particularly compassionate with children, women and other individuals society scorned. He was trying to show us that all people, not just privileged men, are God's children, and we can go God-direct, so to speak, by being 'like him'- prayerful, generous, compassionate, kind, and full of Light.

What tools did Jesus leave us? The ritual he introduced at the Last Supper was one. What do you think Jesus meant when he said: "Take this bread and eat it. This is my body, which will be given up for you. Take this wine and drink from it. It is my blood, which will be shed for you. It is the blood of the new and everlasting covenant"? Why do you think he had his disciples eat and drink something to demonstrate how they could get Christ Consciousness into them?

In Buddhism, the sutra describes the Five Guides of Propagation. One states, Teach According to the Time, another states Teach According to the People's Capacity. Jesus must have known, two thousand years ago, he could only explain Light by giving examples of behavior. He explained people should be kind, which is an outward gesture, but he also wanted them to turn inward, seeking the source of kindness and love. If you eat "his body" and drink "his blood", the substance goes into the back of your mouth, down your throat and esophagus, as close as something can possibly get to the Shushumna, or core of Light running through us. It was a good example, since people eat and drink often. Bringing in the Light was such a new concept that the body needed to be reminded frequently.

I think the primary message from Jesus was each person has the ability to communicate directly with God, by opening the crown chakra and letting Light in. During his time, that was not happening for the average person, and his arrival marked a new phase of development when people were initiated into the process of bringing in Light. If you stand up straight and hold your hands out, it's a cross. That's the path the Light takes. And right where the two lines intersect would be where our heart is, hence the importance of opening the heart chakra. So, I believe the sign of the cross is another reminder for people to run Light through their bodies.

Our Light body is superimposed on, or inside of, our physical body. Imagine a core of Light, like a neon tube, in front of your spine, that comes in through the top of your head (at the fontanel, or the baby's "soft spot"), goes right through the center of your head and body, down to the root of your spine, then splits off and goes down both legs and out the bottoms of your feet. The Light also goes down both arms and out the palms of your hands. Along the core, there are centers called chakras, where the Light comes out. Sometimes chakras can be too open or completely closed, and this can negatively affect your well-being. Often, because life is so mental, and because of physical trauma sustained in life, people tend not to bring the Light all the way down to their feet.

All you need to do to begin to activate and care for your Light body is intend to open the crown chakra, the one at the top of your head. If you've ever wondered how God gets in, that's the place. I noticed at Catholic Church, people bow their heads and the priest makes the sign of the cross right at that spot. Have you ever wondered why he does that? Whether the priest realizes it or not, I believe it is a suggestion to the body to bring in Light.

You may have noticed that the Star of David is two triangles, one inverted and one upright. It is actually an ancient symbol called a Merkhaba. The upright triangle represents earth or matter or male, and the inverted triangle represents the Spirit World or God or female. Perhaps it expresses humankind's desire to be one with God. I believe the Merkhaba represents the human body at its current stage of development. We are a perfect mix of matter and spirit, of earth and God energies. When we ground, we balance ourselves.

Bringing in the Light is the second part of a two-part grounding process. You first need to establish grounding cords from the base of your spine to the center of the earth and bring the earth energy all the way through your body and out the top. Ideally, you would be sitting up straight while you do this. There are many ways to ground. You can imagine tree roots growing out of your feet into the ground, or other similar things. But because we do a lot of clearing work, we like to use many grounding cords. We use a detailed grounding technique (See Chapter 11) before every psychic healing session and Reiki treatment. It really puts you in the Zone. You can change and replace your grounding cords in the morning and at night, since we people process stuff during our sleep as well as in waking hours.

Once you are grounded, sit and let the Light download for a while. The Light contains all the information you will ever need. Here is where you will find absolute truth. You can focus on areas of pain, bringing Light in until the pain goes away. You can send love to others, to the planet, to your enemies. You can intend to scan your body for "cords" other people may have attached to you, and intend to remove those cords, so your space is your own and you are not being influenced by anyone. (For example, a person who is in a relationship with you, who wants more of your attention, or is angry at you, may have cords going into one of your chakras.) You can do all kinds of things when you have time. When you don't have time, the grounding exercise will set you up for the day. You should feel more in rhythm with life, more peaceful, more expanded. In that place, it is easy to remember we are completely supported by the Universe.

From this place, plugged into the Divine Force, our intentions for healing go into the Collective Consciousness of Humanity and begin to heal everyone. Every minute you can spend communing with God or the Oneness, you are making a significant improvement of the condition of the world. It is without a doubt the fast track to attaining world peace.

ೞ

In many churches and in the media, there is a pervasive message of fear and limitation, especially now with the wars in the Middle East. The Self/Other and Good/Evil polarities are being reinforced. A divided people is easily conquered and manipulated. Many Christian churches teach people that energy healers are really evil persons who are acting for Satan, and putting "evil" into you. I guess that's what people thought of Jesus when he first came on the scene, too. I am hoping people have evolved a bit with regard to healing.

I am a Certified Reiki Master and I believe the Reiki energy is supremely spiritual and miraculous in nature. Some folks are put off simply by the name of it. Reiki is a foreign word.

Christian friends immediately become suspicious, and close down when I mention it. Some say they are taught to suspect anyone who is trying to put energy into them. I've actually seen workbooks promoting 'spiritual warfare' from what I would consider radical Christian sects that say meditation is an invitation to be possessed by Satan. They feel the same way about any alternative form of healing. What was Jesus doing at Gethsemane? Wasn't he meditating? He was communing with God. What's evil about that? Wasn't he always healing people simply by being in their presence? Didn't he say we could be like him?

But when I ask if they do laying-on-of-hands at church, their faces brighten up and they say, "yes." Some even go on to explain to me some members of their church speak "in tongues." Some of their church members fall into a strange trance and look as if they are having some sort of a seizure. I can't help wondering, why don't they find those things frightening? Outside the church walls, if someone goes around jabbering unintelligible sounds, they would be taken straight to the psychiatric hospital. Why is it okay to be "possessed" in the church by some unseen force that reduces someone to a lurching, convulsing mass on the floor? Why would they assume it is safe simply because they are inside the church? It's okay to have a group of regular folks put their hands on you and pray for your healing out loud, but it isn't okay to go to a trained practitioner? I don't get it.

People are familiar with the concept that you can be healed with prayer and intention. Unfortunately, as in the nature of religious belief itself, they allow themselves to be convinced one way is okay, but another way is not. Most alternative healers I have met were undeniably on a spiritually evolved path. Alternative healers may choose not to be bound by specific religious dogma, because they want to be available to anyone who seeks help. They expose themselves to the world, at the risk of being persecuted, in hopes someone will come to them for healing, and for lessons in self-healing. For thousands of years, human villages relied on herbal and energy healers and midwives to take care of their medical needs with great success, until the church came along and labeled them instruments of the Devil. What was the motivation behind that, do you think? I guess it's easier to control people who feel they cannot take care of themselves.

☙

The intent to be healed comes from the individual in question. If someone is *seeking* healing, then I am here to offer self-clearing tools, an energetic boost (Reiki), and the idea they can change their circumstances, symptoms and outlook. I have noticed people want to feel better, but there is an innate aversion to facing pain. If you reveal to them it is a doorway rather than a destination, they tend to get a sense of hope, and summon up the strength to view healing as an exciting journey rather than an ordeal in which they must "relive" all their suffering. One of the most important aspects of beginning this process is to find your 'witness' or 'neutral observer.' One needs to be able to step back a bit, out of the drama, in order to view the larger picture and see the correct path. Being in your witness allows you to view the painful drama or spin without being consumed by it.

Because I am a Scorpio, it is very appealing to me to know the 'inside story' or find the 'original cause,' like an investigator. I think that is why I really loved and appreciated Buddhism when it came along. It is truly the inside story. And I love Ayurveda too, because it is the "how to" of spirituality - learning about your light bodies, chakras, auras, and the interaction of energies between the cosmos and the human energy field. Both of those ancient teachings are profound beyond measure.

After a while, one comes to view all events as, not only part of the drama of living within the polar spin but, clues to the bigger picture. And I believe one's emotions are the biggest clues of all. One of my mantras is 'follow your heart.' After all, the goal is to find yourself in the 'expanded heart.' To do that, you must learn to transcend the limiting spin of the victim/tyrant, male/female, scarcity/abundance polarities of the human dynamic. The Law of Attraction bears this out. You can't open your heart if you are always feeling victimized, or waiting to be deceived, or expecting to be poor. Your 'emotional set point' as they say, is your hint to your overall state. Once you express your intent to be joyful and abundant, you take steps to get there, and monitor your emotions to determine whether you are making any progress.

In new age spirituality, it is postulated there is no such thing as 'here and there.' And in addition, time is not linear, ergo there really is no such thing as past, present and future. Therefore whatever has happened in the 'past' is happening right now, and can be remedied "now." That's the beauty of healing energetically. In the Buddhist scripture it says, and I am paraphrasing, "If you wish to know the causes you made in the past, simply look at the condition of your life now." And then my brand of Buddhism goes on to teach you how to go about dissolving those 'past life' causes so you can be happy and healthy NOW. It is a daily practice, and the beneficial effects run deep.

૭૪

The issue of free will came up one day in an email conversation about spirit attachment, and I was surprised by my response. Here's how the conversation went. She said,

"Free Will cannot be taken from you. You cannot be possessed without giving the entity permission to take your body."

I could just feel how conditioned a response that was. How could she know that? Here is my response. Right or wrong, it was how I felt when I read it.

"I have spent 14 years helping people rid themselves of spirits they picked up while under general anesthesia, and by many other circumstances. So, for the most part, I do not find your statement to be true in my experience. Many people are walking around with spirits attached to them. They wonder why they don't feel right, and medical answers do not help them.

"I think it's unfair to place such a burden of responsibility on the afflicted. That's like saying a raped woman "asked for it" or an abused child gave permission to be violated. It's that mentality that led to the Witch Trials and the Inquisition. I can't buy it. Sorry. Perhaps I misunderstood you?"

On a karmic level, one can say, and I have said it during my own recovery from the abusive marriage, we *do* create everything that happens to us. And with the recent discovery of the Law of Attraction, it is said, indeed, everything that comes into our experience is by our own invitation. But consciously, many people do not understand how that comes about, and so when someone makes a comment like that, it sounds like blame. Another Law of the Universe is - everything changes from moment to moment because we are creatures engaged in manifestation. If that is true and, for some unremembered reason, one chooses to be possessed, why then can't it also be true the same person manifests someone to come along and free him or her?

Maybe the possession experience carried a lesson or some leftover karmic debt, but it doesn't mean the person should remain possessed, and it doesn't mean I am interfering with that person's destiny by being willing to clear them of spirits. If we followed that logic, no one should ever go to a doctor. If you're sick, you're sick. "Don't go get medicine, if you're meant to get better you will. If you're meant to die, you will." "If man was meant to fly, God would have given him wings." We left this extremely limited thinking behind long ago.

I really think the possession experience has more to do with energetic vulnerability and a lack of understanding on the part of those who would poison us into unconsciousness in order to perform a lucrative surgery, or those who would drink or drug themselves into a stupor, not realizing they are leaving their energy bodies open and vulnerable. We are more than our physical bodies. We have a protective energetic force field around our bodies, called the aura, and it can be penetrated by the above-mentioned means, as well as traumatic events – shocking and painful experiences. Because this is an energetic situation, it is logical energetic healing can provide the solution. But we have been conditioned to fear the unseen, and leave that kind of work to religious entities who, unfortunately, still subscribe to ancient and often incorrect beliefs about the nature of possession. After all, priests are people too. They too are limited by powerful superiors and manipulated by fear, just like the rest of us.

Still, some people are conflicted about seeking energy healing. Somehow they feel it runs counter to spirituality. They are afraid to open up to someone who is putting energy into them. Yet they willingly put manufactured drugs into their bodies that change their brain function, moods, digestive system and even their physical being. They blindly listen to the medical industry that peddles procedures and tells them they should allow themselves to be poisoned into unconsciousness with gas, and then cut open with a very sharp knife, and have parts of their bodies removed! They even allow their children to be drugged and cut open. Yet they are afraid of energy healing. I guess energy healers don't have enough advertising time on prime time television…

We have been conditioned for millenia to accept and look to intermediaries (priests and the medical industry) between us and the Source of All That Is, despite our having been given a clear message by Enlightened Beings like Jesus who said we could all be 'like Him.' When it comes to dealing with the invisible we are accused of being blasphemous if we dare to take care of ourselves, and told it is the domain of the Church. But if Jesus was telling us the truth and we can be like Him, and he was 'casting out' demons and doing spontaneous healings, why can't we?

I have found out by experience many of the beliefs handed down over the centuries simply cannot be true. I have concluded people have been bound by fear, to be rendered helpless, so powerful and not necessarily spiritually enlightened entities like powerful Churches can continue to hold sway over millions. What if there is no such thing as Satan, Sin or Evil? What if there is nothing to fear but human error? What is there that Love cannot cure?

In our psychic sessions we found, that by inventing beliefs about who should go to heaven and who shouldn't, the Catholic Church in particular caused millions of cases throughout history of people not going to the Light like they should have. Those striving to be spiritually correct believed what the church said, and millions upon millions of people were condemned or sent to "limbo" and "purgatory." People were accused of being Heretics and Witches, and those non-believers along with the unbaptized, victims of religious wars and suicide victims, were condemned by Church officials as being unworthy of entering heaven. Because the beliefs were in place before the people died, in spirit, those people were afraid to even try to go to the Light. Or they stayed behind with the desire to correct a gross injustice. Their beliefs transcended life and death. So, if they didn't go to heaven, where did they go? They hung around the earth plane, haunting their persecutors, staying with their families, prolonging the agony of grief because their loved ones could still perceive their presence. And their symptoms, attitudes and anguish stayed behind as well.

My partner and I have sent the spirits of the so-called unworthy to the Light, and according to Patty, they were not kicked out. Why would a supreme being be limited by mere mortal judgment and beliefs based on the desire to control the masses? I always thought the opposite of faith is fear, yet the dominant Christian religions are heavily imbued with fear – of sinning, of the devil, of going to hell if you don't do what the church says. Those beliefs actually interrupt the connection with the Divine. It is deeply suspect that spiritual advisors would intentionally try to prevent folks from connecting with God. For them it's about power and control, not faith.

Recently Ode magazine featured an article about the Catholic Church reversing its stance in this area. Volume 5, Jan/Feb

2007, entitled "Throwing open the gates of limbo: A Vatican reform stirs conflicting emotion." It reads in part,

"The Vatican has decided to drop the concept of limbo, the place where souls of children who died before they were baptized were said to go. The news prompted some to respond with scorn and mockery, while others experienced pain and anger. The latter group included faithful Catholic mothers and fathers who, in addition to the loss of their newborn, had faced the grief of believing their children would not enter the kingdom of heaven. If that was no longer the case, it must never have been the case, and had been nothing but a cruel fabrication that had caused great anguish."

I found this article too.

Fri Apr 20, 2:21 PM ET

VATICAN CITY (Reuters) - *The Roman Catholic Church has effectively buried the concept of limbo, the place where centuries of tradition and teaching held that babies who die without baptism went.*

In a long-awaited document, the Church's International Theological Commission said limbo reflected an "unduly restrictive view of salvation."

The 41-page document was published on Friday by Origins, the documentary service of the U.S.-based Catholic News Service, which is part of the U.S. Conference of Catholic Bishops.

Pope Benedict, himself a top theologian who before his election in 2005 expressed doubts about limbo, authorized the publication of the document, called "The Hope of Salvation for Infants Who Die Without Being Baptised."

The verdict that limbo could now rest in peace had been expected for years. The document was seen as most likely the final word since limbo was never part of Church doctrine, even though it was taught to Catholics well into the 20th century.

"The conclusion of this study is there are theological and liturgical reasons to hope infants who die without baptism may be saved and brought into eternal happiness even if there is not an explicit teaching on this question found in revelation," it said.

"There are reasons to hope that God will save these infants precisely because it was not possible (to baptize them)."

The Church teaches that baptism removes original sin, which stains all souls since the fall from grace in the Garden of Eden.

"NO NEGATION OF BAPTISM"

"The document stressed that its conclusions should not be interpreted as questioning original sin or "used to negate the necessity of baptism or delay the conferral of the sacrament."

"Limbo, which comes from the Latin word meaning "border" or "edge," was considered by medieval theologians to be a state or place reserved for the unbaptized dead, including good people who lived before the coming of Christ.

"People find it increasingly difficult to accept that God is just and merciful if he excludes infants, who have no personal sins, from eternal happiness, whether they are Christian or non-Christian," the document said.

"It said the study was made all the more pressing because "the number of nonbaptised infants has grown considerably, and therefore the reflection on the possibility of salvation for these infants has become urgent."

"The commission's conclusions had been widely expected.

"In writings before his election as Pope in 2005, the then Cardinal Joseph Ratzinger *made it clear he believed the concept of limbo should be abandoned because it was "only a theological hypothesis" and "never a defined truth of faith."*

"In the Divine Comedy, Dante placed virtuous pagans and great classical philosophers, including Plato and Socrates, in limbo. The Catholic Church's official catechism, issued in 1992 after decades of work, dropped the mention of limbo."

Just where *is* limbo, I wonder? Well, now we know it never existed. The church made it up. Where did all the souls go who believed for hundreds of years they would not be welcomed through the gates of heaven, according to the Catholic Church? Are they hanging around the earth plane, with their families? Are they at the bar? On the battlefield or in the hospital where they died without Last Rites? Lying in their graves in the cemetery, waiting for some sympathetic psychic sensitive to come along and say hello? They are stuck in the magnetic pull of the victim/tyrant polarity. Their beliefs and their traumatic experience keep them here.

To make matters worse, the Church also claimed the exclusive right to be experts in spirit depossession, making people feel too frightened to try and help themselves and jump through incredible hoops in order to see if the Church would help them. It's ironically reminiscent of modern bad governments who create a huge problem, build a frightening mystique around it, blame someone else for causing it, claim to be the only ones who can fix it, then charge an astoundingly high price for doing so, exerting absolute authority and allowing millions to suffer indefinitely.

03

I don't know why my life's path led me to this. I must have chosen it before I got here. My upbringing in a haunted house, the suicide of my brother, the loss of so many of my loved ones, my family's deep connection with Catholicism and all the other defining elements of my life have led me here, to the person I have become. It must be by spiritual design. I am constantly seeking to be a better person, wife and mother. I do not engage in hurtful behaviors. I am bearing the mantle of responsibility of cleaning up the mess the Church has made, like the Peace Corps cleans up after the wars the US wages. I clean up energetic debris, help lost ones find their way home, show people how to rebuild their lives, and I educate.

My psychic partner Patty has seen that there is a thick layer of discarnate souls around the planet, and their presence here interferes with the living, and keeps certain limiting, fear-based patterning in place. No matter how the discarnate souls got there, it became apparent to us if they were free to move on, our living clients would be freed from debilitating symptoms, and the world would be free of another bit of fear-based energy that keeps the cycle of Victim/Tyrant in place for all of us. I have ultimate compassion for the stuck spirits as well as the hosts, and I feel doing this work contributes to the eventual realization of world peace. When we living human beings are no longer influenced by a heavy layer of frightened, angry, deceived, victimized, confused spirits of former human beings, it will be much easier to make sensible, heart-based decisions, easier to have trust and unconditional love for all humanity.

While working with Patty, I saw countless combinations of spirit attachment, multiple attachment, intermittent possession, past life attachments and early childhood trauma containing residuals of the tyrant still in the host's energy field. In some cases it was difficult to tell whether we were viewing a past life, or an attached spirit. We realized, during several years of clearing people it almost doesn't matter. As Patty put it, "the stories are just window dressing on all this energetic stuff."

In terms of past lives and spirit attachment, even though it seems exciting to sit with a psychic and find out who the players are and who did what to whom, the bottom line is to free yourself of those draining and debilitating bonds, so you can have complete access to all of your personal energy and not be influenced by fears and other negative emotions having nothing to do with the life you are consciously living. The key to perfect health is free flowing energy. And one key to free flowing energy is to dissolve traumatic blockages by claiming your space and doing energy healing.

I now view all of life as some sort of patterning. Some of it we brought with us from past lives (karma). Some patterning (as in the case of haunted houses or areas) we match up with, probably for reasons of karma or sustained trauma. We become susceptible for one reason or another. Trauma is a giant magnet.

Because I believe we are all One anyway, I choose not to be limited by the constraints of this or that religion. After decades of faith, spiritual practice and study, I feel I have a good understanding of the workings of human life. The job now, in order to relieve suffering and experience joy in life, is to go in on the energetic level and dismantle the patterning that is being held in place by traumatic experience. Trauma after trauma makes our patterning rigid, and after a while, we find ourselves restricted, limited, ill. Beliefs limit us, as well. I have come to believe we must do all we can to keep our light bodies clear, so we don't manifest illness, and clearing spirits is a very important service I can do for individuals toward that end.

Suicide and Spirit Attachment

"A GREAT NUMBER of unaccountable suicides are due to the obsessing or possessing influence of earthbound spirits. Some of these spirits are actuated by a desire to torment their victims; others, who have ended their physical existence as suicides, find themselves still alive, and, having no knowledge of a spirit world, labor under the delusion that their self-destructive attempts have failed and continue their suicidal efforts.

When these intelligences come in contact with mortal sensitives, they mistake the physical bodies for their own, and impress the sensitives with morbid thoughts and instigate them to deeds of self-destruction.

The fate of a suicide is invariably one of deepest misery, his rash act holding him in the earth sphere until such time as his physical life would have had a natural ending."

Dr Carl Wickland, <u>Thirty Years Among the Dead</u>

People think suicide runs in families. It does, but not necessarily for genetic reasons. After my mother died, it was left to me to empty our Long Island home and sell it. She made me promise never to throw anything away without first looking at it. Needless to say, it took me several months to get the house ready to sell. When I found a box of family photos and memorabilia, I was introduced to my grandmother Jeraldine. She had been my mother's mother, and had died when my mother was 17 years old. There were scraps of poetry, sketches, and many photographs. As I gazed at one particular picture of my grandmother in her teens, I got the chills when I realized the amazing resemblance to my oldest brother Sean. It may as well have been a photo of my deceased brother, wearing turn of the century clothes, a long wavy wig and hat. The hair was the same texture, almost black, shiny and wavy. The eyes were deep with mystery and sorrow.

My grandmother Jeraldine, and my brother Sean. She died in 1937 at 42, he died in 1973 at age 22, same cause of death

My mind went back to the stories my mother told me about her mother. Jeraldine was the youngest of the Sullivan clan. I remember noticing in the genealogy information there had been a baby born after her, who died after only a day or so. There were several children in the family who died within a year, or at a young age. From a Claim Your Space perspective, this is an important factor to keep in mind.

There was also an older brother who experienced a botched ulcer surgery, became addicted to medicinal drugs and depressed before he died. He and his wife had come down from Canada, interested in an entrepreneurial opportunity manufacturing candy from Cactus. They lived with my grandparents, and later the widowed Ning - probably named by my infant mother or toddler Uncle Mark – stayed with Jeraldine and Leo after the death of her husband. I found several photos, before and after Uncle Jack's death.

Left, "Uncle Jack" with bride "Ning."
Jeraldine, right, before her brother Jack's death

The folks came down from Canada for the funeral.
See wisp in foreground – Is it Uncle Jack in the photo?

Jeraldine, after. She changed a lot...

Any of these people might have stayed behind and become attached to a sibling. It can be a concern, especially with the newborns, because there may not have been a funeral ceremony. For centuries, in Catholic tradition, if your baby dies before being baptized, it goes to some place called limbo. The Vatican recently admitted there really is not such a place, but think what torture this belief caused for devout Catholics such as my relatives. What we have found is, due to the beliefs of the parents and confusion on the part of the newborn, the baby will tend to stay with the family. If for any reason a deceased member of the family chooses to stay in the physical plane rather than go to the Light, someone becomes the host, and assumes the moods, attitudes and personality traits of the deceased.

The more I focused on these possibilities, the more I realized it was probably the brother, Uncle Jack, who became attached to my grandmother Jeraldine. He probably didn't want to leave behind his young bride, so stayed in my grandparent's home with his very sad wife. It would have been logical – if he attached himself to his sister, he could sit across the table from his lovely young wife, and "be" with her, sharing a cup of tea, etc. Meanwhile, my grandmother would have assumed his depression, drug addiction and perhaps a desire to be uninhibited.

Back to the photo I was looking at, of my grandmother. I remember my mother telling me how she was very intelligent and sensitive, a poet and writer, and how she had died in 1937, at the age of 42, of alcohol and barbiturate poisoning. She'd had a contentious relationship with my grandfather. On one hand, sometimes it helps to investigate details in hopes of finding reasons why or evidence someone might have had a spirit attached. In this case, because it was long ago, it's all speculation anyway. She could have had the spirit of a deceased brother or a newborn sibling attached to her. For one reason or another, she seemed dark and brooding. On the other hand, maybe none of it matters, as long as you take the steps to clear yourself and your loved ones. By clearing yourself, you are also clearing ingrained family and cultural patterning, as well as trauma that accumulated along the way.

I'm investigative and analytical by nature, so I tried to piece it together by looking at photos, letters and newspaper articles. My grandparents left Canada together right after their marriage in 1917, traveled to Montana and then Texas, following newspaper jobs and oil business opportunities.

They were both journalists, and my grandfather had a law degree. Within a few years, they had bought a place in Miami, which appeared to be hopping, as well as a place in Fort Worth, Texas. Their babies, my mother and uncle, were nursed by a black nanny named Lulu. I noticed, in the many photos, my grandparents were never smiling, even in photos with the children.

My grandparents worked hard and partied hard, during the Roaring '20's, when Granny boots and flapper dresses were all the rage. According to reports from older relatives, Jeraldine had been prescribed barbiturates for her painful bunions, and continued drinking while on that medication. Their marriage broke up when the children were five and seven years old, and my grandfather tried to get custody. Jeraldine brought the kids back to Canada and put my mother in St Mary's, where she was nurtured, raised really, by Sister Theodore of Rome and other relatives.

My Mom with her Aunt

Her brother, my Uncle Mark, went to St. Boniface. The pain of being separated from her parents and her only brother in early childhood must have been a heavy burden for my mother.

My grandmother died when my mother was 17 years old. My mother never got to know her mother well, since my mother had spent her childhood at the boarding school, and summers in the country with an aunt. Feelings of abandonment must have colored my mother's entire life, in a complicated way, since her mother was actually alive during her childhood, but didn't behave as a typical mother. Perhaps it was due to the shame of the separation and divorce. I don't know. Perhaps in the staunch Catholic family, her action of leaving her husband put my grandmother in the position of "black sheep." Perhaps my grandmother was a severe alcoholic and drug addict, and really wasn't capable of raising her own children. I don't know. My mother always put a positive spin on her childhood and upbringing, but every day must have been laced with a deep, longing sorrow.

Some event triggered my grandmother's early death. Here's what I think happened. My grandfather announced his impending marriage to another woman. My grandmother went to see him. She traveled by train from Winnipeg, Canada, to Chicago, Illinois, in order to have dinner with him. That was a long way in 1937. She may have pitched a reunion plea during dinner, and he said no. After all, they had been separated for 14 years, divorced for ten. The next morning, my grandmother was found dead in her hotel room. She was 42. The cause of death was overdose of barbiturates and alcohol. Was it suicide? The ultra Catholic family sure never called it that. They said she must have forgotten she took her nightly dose of pain medication, and took some more. It was accepted within the family as an accidental death.

Fast forward to more recent memories of my brother, who took his life in 1973. He too was poetic, intelligent, sensitive and very melancholy. My mother told me, while she deeply loved all of her five children, when she hugged him as an infant, she felt as if they were melting together, or their souls were merging.

My brother Sean, age seven

My brother's life was laced with emotional agony. He was depressive for as long as I knew him. Mind you, he had good reason to be. My father had been abusive beyond description. When Sean was 5 years old, he and the other children had just witnessed my father attacking my mother in the kitchen; my mother lying in a pool of milk on the floor, crying in agony after my father had used his military training to hurt her by squeezing her pressure points in the neck and other areas.

After my father walked away, five year old Sean rushed to her and said, "I can't wait until I grow up, so I can kill him for you, Mommy!" That was just one incident in a swirl of seemingly endless horrors they experienced while living in our childhood home, the Vortex of Hell. Incidentally, about 25 years later my mother developed a particularly aggressive form of cancer, and the first tumor manifested under her chin, at the "pressure point" where my father used to inflict his torture on her.

By the time my brother Sean was barely a teenager, he had discovered the solace of alcohol. Then came drugs. Sean became known as the black sheep of our family. After the failed suicide attempt by gunshot to the abdomen at age 17 or 18, Sean required massive abdominal surgery, and was given morphine in the hospital for several weeks. After his release, his morphine prescription ran out, and, desperately addicted, he sought an alternative. He found heroin. The next few years were hell for my family, particularly my brother and mother, as his addiction grew out of control. I got sent away to the safety of a convent (more patterning) while my brother was put in a recovery facility. For a short time, there was a glimmer of hope after he graduated from the Methodone program and found a job. But then the Radio Shack incident occurred.

Because of the Methodone program, he had been educated in toxicity levels. He knew how much alcohol combined with Methodone would kill him. He went home to say goodbye, took the pills and went to sleep, never to wake again. My mother had telephoned the physician in charge of the Methodone program, informing him my brother was suicidal, and how much of the drug she thought he had ingested. The doctor's advice was "Let him sleep it off." After my brother died, my mother took the doctor to court. We watched him pay off the coroner in the hallway, and the coroner never appeared to testify. Essentially, there was no coroner's report. The court determined, lacking any proof, and in a situation of my mother's word against the word of a doctor, the doctor's preposterous suggestion must have been true. The court decided at some time in the night, after my brother had passed out and my watchful mother had dozed momentarily, my brother must have gotten up and taken more pills. Sound familiar? The same thing had been said about my grandmother.

I noticed the dates of their deaths, 1937 and 1973.

I am realizing the depths of my mother's despair were much deeper than I had ever realized as a child. She was completely devastated after the death of my brother. And that is understandable. But can you imagine what it must have been like for her to hear those words twice in her life? "He (or she) must have gotten up and taken some more pills." So much blame is implied in that statement. She lost her mother and her oldest son in identical ways. Both incidents were heavily layered with shame and embarrassment, the kinds of things "good" families don't talk about. But bottling it up certainly wasn't the solution. Unresolved patterning only continues, causing more suffering and untimely death.

As I looked through that box of memorabilia in 1982, everything I was looking at reminded me of my brother – my grandmother's physical features, her melancholy mood, her poetic ability and tendency to seek solace in drugs and alcohol. I was only 20 at the time, but, as I held that photo in my hands I found myself concluding my grandmother and my brother must have been one and the same soul. I felt the soul in question had failed in its attempt to set things right. It had succumbed to old patterning. And that pattern was still out there, waiting for its next victim. If there was something to be done about it, I wanted to be the one to do it. That feeling led me down the path of seeking knowledge of the invisible side of life through studying metaphysics and practicing Buddhism. I followed that path from age eleven to the present.

I began looking for the original cause of suicidal depression in my lineage. Perhaps in the end, a genetic flaw could have been the cause. But knowing what I know now, I exhaust every energetic possibility before I settle for a medical explanation. Your medical symptoms can belong to a spirit who is attached to you, and they can vanish as soon as you get cleared. So, determining depression or any other disease is hereditary can be dangerous, in my opinion, because a person simply accepts the diagnosis, and gives up trying to get better. But I didn't know that at the time. In my desperate search to understand what happened to my family, I was about to stumble upon one dynamic that sets up root causes of people's suffering.

Since I read, in Gary Leon Hill's 2005 book, People Who Don't Know They're Dead, about the concept of nesting - when the spirit of a suicide victim goes to another person who then becomes suicidal - I have been forced to consider another theory about the connection between my grandmother and brother. Perhaps my grandmother felt familiar to me because she had been attached to my brother Sean his entire life. Perhaps they weren't the same soul reincarnated after all... That realization caused me to remember my mother's comment about how she felt a merging when she hugged Sean as an infant. She said she had never experienced that feeling with any of the other children. She seemed to feel guilty about it, because the experience felt to her like their souls were merging and she probably should have felt that close to all her children. It was one of those indelible moments, and thankfully she shared it with me when she was on her deathbed.

Perhaps, if my grandmother committed suicide, she knew based on her staunch Catholic upbringing she wouldn't be allowed into Heaven. Or even if her death had been accidental as the relatives maintain, she may have decided to linger. What a tragedy, if one died by one's own actions, without intending to? Where would the spirit of a depressed, religiously condemned mother go - to her youngest child, perhaps? To the one who would suffer feelings of abandonment the most as a result of her loss? Sounds logical to me. Perhaps my grandmother merged with my mother, and stayed with her until my brother Sean was born. He had all my grandmother's features. Perhaps that memorable moment of merging my mother referred to on her deathbed was the moment the spirit of my grandmother passed from my mother to my brother.

ରେ

People talk about genetic tendencies, but I think there can be something else going on. My brother died at the age of 22, when I was eleven. When I was 26, I had my first child, a son whom I named Sean. I had recently befriended Patty, and I went to her because my son, at the tender age of 6, was making suicidal comments. He was very sad and having unsuccessful social interactions at school.

One day after school, as I was putting the key in the door, my son said, "I want to go home." I got goose bumps from head to toe.

I said, "What do you mean? We are home."

He shook his head, pointing upward and repeated, "I want to go home, to be with the Angels."

My son Sean, age seven

My son's early childhood suicidal depression threw me into a spiritual crisis. I was determined to put an end to the patterning that had plagued my family for generations. I chanted with my whole heart, my whole being, to find the root cause of all this suffering, and put an end to it, without losing my son's life. If I had lost him, it would have been the end of me, as well. I was desperately determined, as they say in

Buddhism, to turn poison into medicine. I was not going to let the spin of patterning claim any more lives if I could help it.

All other details in my life took a back seat. I took traditional steps, like counseling and having him evaluated by both a psychologist and a psychiatrist. After a 30 minute visit and the psychiatrist's short interview with my six year old son, Sean was diagnosed with suicidal depression and a non specific, moderate mood disorder. The psychiatrist prescribed a frightening drug called Nortriptylene. Since Sean was so young, the doctor prescribed it in liquid form. The liquid form had a significant amount of alcohol in it. I had serious misgivings, considering his family history on both sides. When I went to the pharmacy to pick up the prescription, the clerk presented me with a huge brown glass bottle. It was at least quart sized. My new husband begged me not to put Sean on the meds. I was conflicted because I knew he needed help, but I was also deeply suspicious of pharmaceuticals after what had happened to my brother and grandmother. We tried it for two days. The medicine changed my little boy so dramatically, it was shocking. We took him off of it.

Meanwhile, as I was chanting for my son, I was seeing the deep patterning in my family's life. The victimization I saw on individual levels was expanded to the family level, then to a cultural level. I realized victimization of the Irish was very deep, ingrained over centuries. Add to that the conditioning heaped on them by the Church. Add to that the 30 year long odyssey my family had in the house on High Street. I realized it was all one big ball of energetic stuff, and with intention, effort, and the workings of the Mystic Law, I might be able to transform the mess into something sacred. I had to. My son's life depended on it.

I sincerely believe my chanting led me to meeting Patty, and she was the key to unlocking the mystery. My sessions with her were by far the most healing experiences I'd ever had. She found the spirit of my suicidal brother attached to me, and sent him to the Light. If the nesting concept is true, the day we released my brother, we may also have released my grandmother, almost 60 years after her passing. I believe my brother's, and perhaps grandmother's, feelings had been influencing both my son and me. When we reconciled my brother's angst and enabled him to move on, a shadow of pain lifted from both of us. Life became brighter after that, more manageable, livable.

☙

One thing innately built into all humans is a strong sense of self-preservation. Any time a person feels like death is a good option, something is very wrong. There are many agencies out there to offer support to suicidal people, but I don't think many of them address the situation from this perspective. After doing this work for so many years, whenever I encounter a suicidal person, spirit attachment is the *first* thing I would suspect and rule out before moving on to other causes and diagnoses. The Claim Your Space™ routine could be offered over the phone on Suicide Hotlines. It can be performed in hospitals, at home, on a webcam, wherever. It seems like a suicidal person needs a helper to get through the clearing, because he or she has almost completely given in to the emotions of the spirit. In essence, the host needs help to convince the spirit of the situation, and the spirit needs help accepting he or she is dead, not a wrongdoer, and deserves to go to the Light, like everyone else. This may fly in the face of long held Catholic tradition, but I believe the firsthand accounts I received from my psychic partner Patty, who watched these suicidal spirits be accepted and welcomed into the Light.

Over time, I have encountered other situations in the realm of suicide. As a Reiki practitioner, I have given treatments to people with chronic pain and terminal illness. On two occasions, the client was suicidal when I arrived for our first treatment. After only one Reiki treatment, each of these suicidal men did a complete turnaround, and began to care about living, and making future plans. In one case, the man's gay partner had died of AIDS, and the man said he felt as if his partner was still with him. So during the Reiki treatment, I had him claim his space. The next time I saw him, he was elated.

His severe neuropathy had disappeared, he was free to walk again, and he had called and spoken to his mother for the first time in ages. His suicidal feelings, physical symptoms and negative relationship with his mother, had apparently all belonged to his deceased partner. When he claimed his space, all of those symptoms disappeared, and he was free to enjoy his life again.

The second situation involved a middle aged man who had been severely abused in childhood. The career path he chose meant he was surrounded daily by sex offenders who had likely also been severely abused in childhood. Not realizing his deepest issues were being triggered daily, the man began to rely more heavily on anti-anxiety medication and alcohol. Over the course of a few years, he went from having hallucinations and panic attacks to suffering from Grand Mal seizures. He was a perfect candidate to be the host of multiple entities, which may have increased his compulsion to drink vast quantities, but it was my opinion the seizures were caused by the combination of pharmaceuticals and alcohol. The day I came to give him a Reiki treatment, it was barely noon, and he was already intoxicated. In fact, he asked me a question, and when I turned to answer him, I noticed he had drifted out of consciousness. When he did speak, he confessed being dead would probably feel better than his daily life.

During the treatment, I could tell he was uncomfortable with the hands-on aspect, probably because of his early childhood abuse. We actually only got half way through the treatment when he jumped up and claimed he was hungry. He was suddenly full of energy. He had told me earlier that eating was difficult, as he had no appetite and became nauseous when he tried to eat. Yet now he wanted to go out to lunch. My cynical mind was thinking he wanted to avoid the rest of the treatment, but at the same time I was very pleased he was eating, and during the meal, he suddenly had ideas about a change in career path. Shortly after our treatment, he went into rehab, went off the Paxil and became sober. His seizures stopped.

More recently, I received an email from a girl in England regarding suicide. I am quite proud of her for having the capacity to understand what was truly going on. She was happy to discover my techniques, and relieved an 'older' person like me could really understand what she and her friends were going through. Here are some excerpts of our email exchanges, two days after Christmas.

"Hello,

"My friend hung herself last year. Ever since, really strange things have been happening. For example, my friends and I were at a friend's house, sitting in her room all talking. We were searching her bedroom for funny stuff when we found a box. Sarah swore she threw it away years ago, but when we opened it up, it had notes we had all written in class to Jenny [the girl who died], and pictures of us all together. Then we felt a strange feeling, like we were being watched or something. So I said jokingly, "Jenny if you're here, let us know." Strange things started to happen like, the door slammed shut and the TV kept flickering, so Sarah said "That could just be a coincidence. We need more, Jenny."

"So we left the room for a bit to get food, but the microwave wasn't working. Sarah went back upstairs and we heard her scream. We all ran up there. Sarah was crying so much, we asked her what was wrong, and she said she had seen Jenny but the rope was still 'round her neck. She waved at Sarah and then she walked through the wall, but Sarah said it looked like some kind of door. Do you think she is lying?

"I am so confused!! It would be a great help if you could tell me."

I responded, "My brother killed himself when I was 11. I found out 20 years later he never went to the Light, but had been hanging around me. Suicide victims can be confused, thinking they're not really dead. Also their religious beliefs may cause them to believe they don't deserve to go to the Light, so they hang around friends and loved ones.

"But this is very bad, because if your friend was depressed, or addicted to alcohol or drugs, you or her other friends or relatives will take on her symptoms, including becoming suicidal.

"Please read "What to do if you think you're being haunted" (See Chapter 11). The best thing you can do for your friend is to tell her she's dead, and send her to the Light. Your lives may depend on it. She responded the same day.

"Although this has made me cry thinking about my friend Jenny, it also made me smile in relief knowing there is someone out there who does know how I feel and isn't just saying they do to make me happy. A huge weight has been taken off shoulders - Thank you x

"You talk about the spirit being around a certain loved one or friend but, in my case, it seems to be a whole bunch of friends, the same people [including me] who she hung around with a lot, went out with, etc. It seems to be some kind of chain, as though she is hanging around one person, being Pam maybe, and then because she is down, others are getting down too? I'm no expert in this, but I really appreciate your help, I'm crying and smiling at the same time.

"Thank you, thank you, thank you!

"I know this sounds stupid but it's such a relief!! This is just what I've been searching for. I would do searches on my computer about suicide to read up on it, but never got what I wanted, just read about other attempted suicides or succeeded suicides. This is what I'm looking for!

"The ceremony? What kind of ceremony is it? Maybe you could send me a message telling me more about this, it would be much appreciated. Send me a message. Thanks once again."

I must have asked her how everyone was doing, explaining one way to tell if her suicidal friend's spirit was still around, was other people would be thinking and acting like the deceased girl.

"No one has been completely happy since it happened - obviously we're not going to be, because of our age and stuff, but thinking about it yesterday, it was 1 year and 5 days. People still say they can't help. Her very best friend now won't eat, didn't have Christmas and is anorexic. She won't come out or do anything. I went through a VERY bad stage, going from size 14 to a 6/8. I've only just managed to get myself to a size 12 and I'm constantly having days where I just want to cry.

"My friends think it's stupid because, whenever I've felt her around I've said, "Oh come on chick, yer dead sweetie, go rest" and stuff like that, and my friends are like, she won't hear you!

"Thank you for taking your time to help, maybe we can get chatting and you can help me alot more and show me things I need to be shown. I will listen to that radio interview tomorrow and I'm going to read your blog. Email me back from this message and I'll let you know!

"Thanks again!"

I replied. "Yes, she will hear you, because I think she is still around. I'm worried about her best friend. It sounds like you're sure she's still around, because you're seeing her, and still having severe grief after a whole year. Was there ever a funeral?

"If you want to find out whether she's still in the earth plane instead of heaven, think about everything she was suffering from, and see if her best friend, or you, or anyone else is now suffering from those same things.

"Did the girl who died (Jennifer?) have an eating disorder?

"Did she stay in her room, like her friend is doing now?

"Perhaps you and your other friends, after reading my blogs (see Chapter 11), can sit together and give her a personal funeral, with just you girls. You need to tell Jenny she died, and you all (especially you and the best friend) need to say the Claim Your Space™ exercise out loud, saying any other person, spirit, etc, does NOT have permission to be in your space and needs to go now.

"Jenny doesn't realize that she's harming her best friend, so you should tell her. And tell her she is perfectly welcome in the light. She is forgiven, but she doesn't need forgiveness, because she will not be judged in the Light. There is only love in the Light.

"I know it's a lot for you young girls to do, but it's better than continuing to suffer. I don't want your friend to starve to death because she has a spirit attached to her.

"I'd be happy to speak to anyone's parents, if you think it's a good idea."

Next day she replied.

"Hey,

"Yes, there was a funeral. I attended only a bit of it because I was too upset to carry on. Pam (her best friend) went to all of it, including the burial. We all go to her grave a few times a month and we speak to her and things like that – don't know if that helps? (Visiting the gravesite may have made them vulnerable.)

"Yeah, I'm pretty sure she's still around and so are a few others. It's hard to tell my mum and dad (well I don't tell my dad, ha ha!) but I tell my mum a lot, though... it seems hard to tell her this because it's just so upsetting and sometimes she just doesn't seem to get it. And anyway, I'm thinking it's more of a friend thing. We said we would get through it together, besides having counseling. But there seems no one in the world who we can talk to who will keep their mouths closed!

"We said we would do this together because adults don't seem to understand. They're always like, "it's just your imagination," but we are sure it's not!

"Jennifer suffered from bullying and very bad family problems. It was such a shock because it was totally unexpected. We knew she wasn't very happy, but we always thought it was just... I don't know, we thought it would be over soon and would all get better, as kids do!

"Then one day we got the news. First we thought it was a sick joke, but then it was confirmed. It was such a shock because we didn't think it was that bad. But she had mentioned to Pam she wanted to do it to herself and Pam thought she was just saying it and wouldn't actually do anything. I myself have had a few chats with Pam, I've been able to get to her and say we really need to chat... She said she's feeling guilty because she could have stopped Jenny. I was saying to her she mustn't blame herself for this because, no matter what, she would have done it, we all know she would have. She was a VERY strong-minded girl!

"Today I'm going to talk to my girls and arrange a date for them all to come 'round. Mum and dad are going out they have said, on that day, to let us have some privacy. I will make cookies and we can all have a little chat and read up on your blogs. Hopefully this way they will see it is important we do things soon before it gets even more out of hand!

"I don't think Pam will come; she doesn't ever want to come out. Although Jennifer used to hide it, Pam doesn't seem to... Although I think she tries to hide it, but it's kind of obvious with her losing all that weight and just being unhappy. I will see what I can do though!

"Us girls, yeah we're young but with this happening so young in life to us, it's made us realize a whole lot more and we have realized if we put our minds to something, we will achieve it and we can do it, but we have to have faith and we have to be able to understand we can do it!

"Again, thank you for your help. I will keep you informed if anything else happens. Much, much appreciated,

"Keep in touch please, I really do value your help."

"Great, you can all get together, but you're not sure about Pam. I think because you are all close friends, you can ask on Pam's behalf that she be cleared. But it would be ideal if you can all go to Pam's house, or if she could be present. I really feel, even though Jenny is floating around a bit, she has mainly settled with Pam.

"Often times, when we have a spirit attached to us, we begin to feel the feelings of the deceased person. When you say Pam feels guilty, I'm thinking it's really Jennifer's guilt about killing herself. It's hard to realize when you're having someone else's thoughts and feelings.

"This is not going to be easy. It's definitely going to be an emotional experience, so bring the Kleenex. But emotion is keeping her stuck, so all of these next things are very important to do. There are things Jennifer needs to express and hear, and you are going to have to do them for her.

"And make sure you don't drink any alcohol before or during this ceremony. Drinking lowers your vibration, and makes you susceptible to spirit attachment.

"One thing you can do on Jennifer's behalf, when you are doing the clearing is to say out loud, 'On behalf of Jennifer (use her last name too), I sincerely apologize to all my friends and family for leaving so suddenly. I really didn't know how it was going to be. Please forgive me.'

"And another thing that seems important, you can say to Jennifer on behalf of her family, "We sincerely apologize for abusing and hurting you. We were very wrong to do that. We love you, and we are very sorry we couldn't be better people. We hope you find love and peace in the Light.'

"Some of the things she needs to hear are, you all forgive her, and she is loved, and she is now free to move on. She feels guilty, and that is one of the things keeping her here. So, you, or whoever the spokesperson is, should say out loud that everyone forgives her, even her family. You should go around the circle, and each person say, 'I forgive you, Jennifer. Please go to the Light.' Bring some fresh cut flowers to the little ceremony.

"Tell Jennifer (out loud) as long as she lingers here, she is harming her friends and family. There is nothing to fear in the Light. There is only love in the Light. And after she goes into the Light, at some point she will get another chance to live in a physical body, and start fresh.

"I wish I could be there to help you. When you're ready, feel free to ask questions."

I didn't hear from her for a few weeks, so I checked in with the English girl whose young friend had committed suicide. I wanted to know if they'd done the ceremony I recommended.

"How did it go?"

"Ahhh, forgot to contact you about it. Sorry! It went very well to be honest... Pam even came... and although it was very emotional we got through it. Thanks for all your help ☺ xx"

This young girl and I may never meet, but I feel good knowing I have given her an effective tool to help her deal with what happened to her friend. She needn't be plagued for life. She can claim her space.

Symptoms

"SPIRITS who are ignorant of having lost their physical bodies often hold firmly in mind the thought of their former physical condition and continue to suffer pain. This "error of the mortal mind" persists until an understanding of transition and spiritual laws is reached, when freedom from ideas of physical limitations is attained.

When spirits who are under this delusion of suffering and disease come into the auras of mortals, their condition is conveyed to the sensitives, and chronic lassitude, pseudo-illness and psychic invalidism result.

These sensitives endure all the pain of the spirits' former physical condition, and ordinary methods of treatment fail to cure, for the only permanent relief is found through the dislodgement of the ignorant entities."

From Thirty Years Among the Dead, p.206, Dr Carl Wickland

Having spirits attached to you can cause panic attacks, anxiety, suicidal tendencies, depression, mood swings, memory loss, weird physical problems, addictions, food and other kinds of obsessions, etc. It is because you take on all the desires, fears, attitudes, appetites, addictions and general health symptoms of the spirits that are attached to you.

We came to these conclusions over the course of 14 years of psychic sessions. Needless to say, we were very relieved when we came across extant documentation to support our findings. We found The Unquiet Dead within the first few years of our work, and I did use Dr Fiore's ideas for having dialogue with the spirit. In our sessions, the dialogue was more interesting, because of Patty's medium abilities. We didn't need to rely on the subject to find out what the spirit was thinking and feeling.

See excerpt from Dr. Edith Fiore's book, The Unquiet Dead.

"Spirit Possession has been reported since ancient times. Is it real?

"Moved by the suffering of patients who came to her with seemingly incurable psychological and psychosomatic problems, noted psychologist Dr. Edith Fiore began to explore beyond the boundaries of traditional psychology and made a startling discovery – a significant number of her patients were suffering from spirit possession, a condition that no amount of orthodox treatment could cure.

"Depression, phobias, addiction – these and other disorders can be caused by spirits who, after death, remained in the physical world as "displaced" persons inhabiting the bodies and minds of those still living. The Unquiet Dead is filled with the case histories of these patients, along with details of Dr Fiore's hypnotherapeutic methods.

"The Unquiet Dead offers a new and fascinating look at the obstacles to peace of mind and spiritual health that can afflict any of us in THIS life."

THE UNQUIET DEAD by Dr. Edith Fiore, 1987

It wasn't until almost the end of our 14 year partnership that one of our clients brought us the book <u>People Who Don't Know They're Dead</u>, by Gary Leon Hill. The book was published in 2005. In it, he names many authors, one of whom was early 20th century psychiatrist, Dr Carl Wickland, who I have quoted and mentioned several times. He developed the specialty of curing severely mentally and emotionally disturbed patients by ridding them of what he called "obsessing spirits." With the good fortune of having a psychic wife, the doctor was quick to realize the spirits of the deceased remain and, when attached to a living human being, can cause all manner of ills. His success rate was astonishing.

Here are some excerpts from Dr Wickland's book.

"The change called 'death,' - the word is a misnomer - universally regarded with gloomy fear, occurs so naturally and simply that the greater number, after passing out of the physical are not aware that the transition has been made, and having no knowledge of a spiritual life, they are totally unconscious of having passed into another state of being.

"Deprived of their physical sense organs, they are shut out from the physical light and, lacking a mental perception of the high purpose of existence, these individuals are spiritually blind and find themselves in a twilight condition—the "outer darkness" mentioned in the Bible—and linger in the realm known as the Earth Sphere. "Death does not make a saint of a sinner, nor a sage of a fool." The mentality is the same as before, and individuals carry with them their old desires, habits, dogmas, faulty teachings, indifference or disbelief in a future life. "As a man thinketh in his heart, so is he." Prov. 23:7.

"Assuming spirit forms, which are the result of their thought life on earth, millions remain for a time in the earth sphere, and often in the environment of their earth lives, still held by their habits or interests. "Where your treasure is there will your heart be also." Matt. 6:21.

From Thirty Years among the Dead, by Carl Wickland

The variations of symptoms are seemingly endless. The situation of spirit possession is complicated, in that we are dealing with multiple layers – any existing symptoms belonging to the host, symptoms belonging to the possessing entity, and symptoms caused as a result of being possessed (fatigue, confusion and memory loss are the most common). Experience has helped me to narrow diagnosis down to "easy recognition." My intuition guides me to these people, or Spirit guides them to me, I'm not sure which, and within their first few sentences, I know whether spirit attachment or traumatic density is causing their problems. It's not very scientific, but it has happened so often, I have come to regard it as a sign. I get goose bumps when they are in the midst of describing their situation to me. And it doesn't matter whether the conversation is in person, on the telephone, or by email. If I get goose bumps, I know the Claim Your Space exercise will help the person I'm talking to.

There are circumstances of ghosts who inhabit your environment, and ghosts who inhabit your body. It's easier to determine there is activity when you can view it in your environment. Nevertheless, the house ghosts can intermittently possess you, and cause you harm, even if they seem to you to be friendly. Often, people sense one of their deceased relatives is visiting and while they are somewhat alarmed they are experiencing paranormal activity, they are reluctant to accept that the situation needs to be remedied. That is, until we begin discussing symptoms.

Possession by Relatives

A woman emailed to say she felt sure there was some invisible presence in her apartment. Whoever it was seemed to be having a good time with her new baby. The baby would turn its head as if watching something, and smile and coo and bat at this invisible thing. Was it spirit guides? The house was 100 years old, and their apartment was above some kind of bar or hotel. Was it inhabited with previous tenants? She added that perhaps it was her grandmother, coming to see her great grand baby. The baby was named after this deceased great grandmother. When I implied she should claim her space and not give the entity permission to be there, she balked.

"Well, if it's grandma, she's welcome here. My grandmother and I were very close, that's why I named the baby after her. I'm happy she's having an opportunity to visit with my baby."

"What symptoms did your grandmother have before she died?" I explained to her how we take on the symptoms of earthbound spirits that are in our energy field.

She became much more attentive, almost alarmed. "She died of a respiratory illness. Both the baby and I have had recurring asthma and bronchitis. Do you really think grandma could be the cause?"

I told her the spirit usually has no idea it is negatively affecting the hosts. Often the spirit doesn't even realize it is deceased. I told her she needed to sit down one day, ground herself and have a talk with grandma, explaining she is no longer in a physical body and she is inadvertently sharing her symptoms with her beautiful new grand baby. She should tell her grandmother to look for the Light, and that someone she knows will be waiting for her. "Reassure her you will never forget her, and perhaps she can come back, but only AFTER she has gone completely into the Light."

※

Another young woman had a long history of hearing voices, and had been diagnosed with a psychiatric disorder. She was also beginning to exhibit symptoms of Multiple Sclerosis. Her symptoms included body pain, tremors and trouble walking. When she was diagnosed with MS, she asked the doctor if the MS would cause her to hear voices. Apparently her own doctor told her, "No. I've known you since you were a little girl. I don't think you're crazy, I think you're being haunted."

This woman had a very long and rambling story to tell about paranormal activity occurring in her apartments on and off over a four year period and through two relationships. The cat and birds would suddenly become very agitated. She would hear a woman screaming, and hear a woman calling her name. The shower curtain disappeared shortly after they put it up, she'd hear banging on walls and the sound of someone sitting on the porch, but nobody was there. Water faucets and light switches would go on and off by themselves. It terrified her husband so much, he left her, and she had to go home and live with her mother.

After she moved back home, the activity subsided. When she met another man and moved into an apartment with him, the activity started up again, with a vengeance. This boyfriend claimed he saw a ghost, an old woman wearing overalls.

One day, while looking at family photos, he pointed to one and said, "That's her! That's the ghost I saw!" It was an Aunt, one of her mother's sisters.

I asked the woman, "How old were you when your Aunt died?"

"10 years old and we were very close."

"Would your Aunt have disapproved of your marriage?"

"Yes."

"Would she have preferred if you were living at home with your mother?"

"Yes"

"What did she die of?"

"Parkinson's."

"Do the symptoms of Parkinson's include tremors, body pain and difficulty walking?"

"Yes." Then she said, "I kinda knew my Aunt always was around me. I had an MRI done the other day and, when I closed my eyes, I pictured her holding my hand and I felt as if she was, too. I think about dying alot and, when I do, I get happy, and I see her in my mind. Even though she died when I was 10, I feel her so much."

Those last comments were serious red flags. I explained to this young woman I thought her Aunt had been attached to her since childhood, and that explained the female voice she had "always" heard. The feeling of being happy if she died is most likely her Aunt's feeling. She said she thinks about dying a lot. It is possible the Aunt doesn't even realize she is dead.

According to the statement by Dr Wickland, it is possible the Aunt continues to feel all of her body pain, etc, and would like it to be over, not realizing she died decades ago. And because she attached herself to her favorite niece, the niece now has all of her Aunt's attitudes and symptoms.

Maybe it was the Aunt who wanted to go and live with her sister (client's mother). Her Aunt would act up when the girl was with an unacceptable man, and calm down when she was back home with her mom. Apparently, her Aunt didn't trust men. In the course of our conversations, the client did mention she really hated being bossed around by men on the job. As I learned more, I realized that feeling probably also belonged to her Aunt. So, you can see how subtly yet profoundly spirit attachment can affect the living.

I explained to her that when we have a spirit attached, we take on their symptoms, and tried to encourage her that even though she'd had an MRI, it is possible the lesions on her brain, and all of her physical symptoms might go away if she claimed her space. I wondered if Parkinson's symptoms include lesions on the brain, like MS. She felt doubtful anything could contradict the results of the MRI. People are so willing to simply accept medical diagnoses and give up! But she said she would try the Claim Your Space™ exercises anyway. When I followed up with her a few weeks later, she stated she had cleared her house and all the activity had stopped. I don't know whether she consciously sent her Aunt away or not, but I hope she decides to try it someday. A situation like this can be very difficult because she has been feeling her Aunt's feelings in addition to her own ever since she was a little girl. People can be gripped with fear and suspicion about claiming their space, not realizing those emotions are not their own.

Sudden onset of unexplainable symptoms makes spirit attachment much easier to recognize. It doesn't always happen that way, but here is one example.

☙

Attached at the Hospital

One of our most profound cases involved a woman who was a caretaker for her diabetic mother. The diabetes caused multiple symptoms that often required trips to the hospital. On one of those occasions, they were in the Emergency Room when a man right next to them, behind the curtain, died suddenly. This man and his family were Spanish-speaking, so the women couldn't determine what he had died of, based on the conversation between the doctor and the man's family. When the tension of the moment receded and the doctor escorted the family out of the room, the woman who became our client, couldn't resist the opportunity to peek behind the curtain and view the deceased man. She had never seen a dead body before.

When she missed a Reiki appointment with me, I called her. I asked, "How are you doing?"

She said, "Well, I'm not feeling very well. I have all the symptoms of Congestive Heart Failure (CHF), but the doctors don't know why."

I asked, "What do you mean?"

She explained that after she left the hospital with her mother, she began to feel very unwell. She developed fluid in her lungs, swollen legs and difficulty breathing. She went back to the hospital and had an EKG, but the results were normal. The doctors had said her thyroid had completely stopped functioning, and she was exhibiting all the symptoms of CHF, but they couldn't say why. The perplexed physicians sent her home with a full strength prescription for thyroid medication.

As she related her story, my goose bumps went into overdrive. I said, "I feel like this is an emergency. When can you come and see us?"

She came over immediately, and we did a session. Patty discovered the deceased man in her aura right away. For a moment I pondered whether there might be a language barrier when dealing with spirits, but it turned out he could understand us just fine. He had died so suddenly, he didn't realize he was dead. When his family walked away, he became alarmed, and approached our client to ask a question. He got stuck in her energy field, and she began to experience the same symptoms that had just killed him. We explained that he had died, and that he should look for the Light. He replied he could see it. We asked if he could see anyone he recognized in the light, and he responded he saw his grandmother. He quietly and sincerely apologized to our client for having caused her any harm, thanked us, and went into the Light.

The session wasn't over yet. I should explain some people are more prone to spirit attachment than others. We speculate there are a few reasons for this. One, psychically sensitive persons tend to be vulnerable, especially if they had ever used drugs or alcohol to alter their consciousness. And two, if a person already has a density in place it slows down the vibrational frequency of their aura and energy field. Oftentimes, Patty has revealed situations that were difficult to differentiate between spirit attachment and past life karma. In some cases, the presentation is the same, and fortunately, so is the cure. This was the case as we continued to view our client.

As an added precaution, after we sent the man to the Light, I asked Patty to view our client's chakras, looking for any "dark spots" or things that obviously didn't belong. Patty stopped at the fifth chakra.

As Patty looked at the dark spot clouding this woman's throat area, she found herself in the midst of one of our client's past life experiences. Patty's specialty always brings her to the end of a life - to the traumatic way in which a particular life was ended - and then we would reconcile anything shown to us. In a past life, our client had died as a young girl, choked nearly to death by her enraged mother. She didn't die immediately, but the extent of the damage was such that she could only swallow liquids, and over time, her life slipped away as she slowly starved to death. As she lay dying, the young girl was very angry her life had been robbed, and that she could no longer enjoy life-giving food. She was also heartbroken that her mother, the person you are supposed to be able to trust the most in the whole world, had tried to kill her. She had felt abandoned, betrayed, helpless.

Our client had some psychic ability, and said she recognized her mother in the past life was one of her brothers in this life. She had always loved to eat in this life, and was chubby in her youth. Weight had always been an issue for her and it now made sense. The brother had teased and tormented her mercilessly during their childhood. She also explained to us that she had suffered from a malfunctioning thyroid for years, and during the latest episode with the CHF symptoms, her thyroid had stopped functioning completely. She had been very low on energy when the spirit attachment incident occurred. She was maxed out on thyroid medication, and there was nothing more the doctors could do for her.

In our unique way, we allowed our client as the young girl, to receive an apology from the mother. The mother expressed sincere remorse that she had allowed her temper to go out of control. She felt terribly guilty she had sentenced her young daughter to a slow death. The young girl tearfully forgave her mother, and that portion of her frozen, abandoned, enraged psyche was freed to go into the Light. Any remaining portion of the guilt stricken mother was also freed to carry on. As Patty watched, the darkness began to dissolve and light began to fill up the 5th chakra. She continued her chakra inspection and, finding everything else in order, ended the session.

Our sat client up and we gave her a cup of tea. Over the next few minutes, we observed the color of her skin changing from gray to pink. Her breathing eased. She called after 48 hours to announce all of her symptoms had gone away. A month later, she called again to say that after a brief stint of feeling unwell, she returned to the doctor, only to be told her thyroid medication was making her feel ill. Her thyroid was functioning normally and she was told to get off the meds completely. Our client had been on thyroid medication for 10 years, having to take ever-increasing doses, and suddenly her thyroid is working perfectly well? She was exhilarated, went on the first completely successful diet in her life, lost 70 pounds in an 8 month period, and began a whole new phase of her life. And her relationship with the abusive brother improved.

ೞ

Invasion During Surgery

One day a woman requested a prayer for her husband.

"Hey there, just wanted to ask you to say a quick prayer for my husband. He is feeling sick and it really worries me. He has a condition that can act up at any time. I am just keeping a close watch, and looking for the signs I need to rush him back to the ER. I got so nervous that now I feel sick. Thanks for taking the time out to read my ramblings."

I replied, "Just to be on the safe side, you could claim his space for him ☺"

"Thank you. By the way, what is claiming? Didn't understand that."

"Whenever someone has a very stubborn illness, one that is not typical or doesn't go away, I suspect negative energies stuck in the body. The energies could be a trapped spirit, or residuals from a traumatic event he may have experienced in this life or a past life. If the illness occurs in a particular part of his body, you may know if he sustained any kind of abuse in his childhood that would have affected him in that area. Or if he ever had surgery and was put under general anesthesia, he could have come home with the spirit of someone who had (and maybe died of) those exact symptoms.

"Even if you're not sure, it doesn't hurt to say the words in the Claim Your Space™ exercise, intending to claim his space, in case there is energy in there that doesn't belong to him. It can't hurt if it turns out there was nothing, but it can help a great deal if he did have something there, and it goes away. Many times, I've seen symptoms vanish when people claim their space.

"Because you're his wife, you can do it on his behalf, and he doesn't even need to be in the room. It's better of course, if he'll sit with you and say the words out loud. When a person says, "My name is _____. I claim my space as my own. Any other person, spirit, entity or energy form does NOT have permission to be in my space and needs to go now." It is my understanding the energy must move.

"In some instances it doesn't happen right away, and then investigation is in order. Like, if its grandma and he's having the same symptoms she had, and she doesn't go away right away because she thinks she's helping by staying around. If a relative is in someone's space, they usually don't realize they're making someone sick. Then, once you think you know who may be sharing his space, you can speak specifically to that person and explain they are dead, and they are unintentionally harming the host."

She replied, "Thank you for sharing your knowledge with me. I will try it tonight. Both my husband and I have had numerous surgeries for obesity, and I have felt extremely weak since my initial surgery. I could never make it out. Why am I weaker and sicker now after all the weight loss? I guess this makes a lot of sense. Thank you."

I added, "If your personality changes or you suddenly desire foods or drinks or things you didn't like before, those are obvious signs of spirit attachment. Lack of energy level is an obvious sign someone could be sharing your space. In the case of couples, if one of you suddenly loses attraction for the other, you might have a spirit of the opposite sex attached to you. Check my exercises in "What to do if you think you're being haunted." (see chapter 11). That one gives many details. The salt bath is very helpful. I'm here if you want to talk about it."

A few days later, she responded.

"Kelly,

"I just wanted to say thank you so much. I have had two major surgeries and was under for a long time. So has my husband. We both feel super fatigued. I even started to wish I was dead. I couldn't take it anymore. I hate being sick. I am not the whiny type, the complainer. Usually if I got sick I would go lay down until it passed. Now after my surgeries, I have even lost my sexual interest, which is weird. I felt like it wasn't me. I can't explain. Well I started thinking hard and long about what you told me and to me it made sense. I mean, I used to be fat and feel as strong as an ox. Now I can't even lift things. I feel like I am 100 years old. My drive was gone. I couldn't even clean my house. I used to be anal retentive about cleanliness and now, I didn't care. Didn't have the energy; didn't have the drive.

"Well, the other day in the kitchen, I thought I fainted. My husband says I was never really out, although I felt like I was out. I remember joking around with him... and then I started to see everything go black. I called him and I thought I said "I'm fainting" 3 times. He says I never said it. I held on to the end of the counter and fell down slowly since I was holding on. I have felt someone in my kitchen before mind you. Other psychics have told me someone is there. I fell to my knees and for a second I could see myself in this darkness... I could hear myself talking but far, far away. It was really strange. It felt like maybe15 seconds of it. Anyhow, my husband helps me up and I come to. Oh, in the darkness it was peaceful. Well, as soon as he starts talking to me I opened my eyes and realized what happened. I started to feel pain in my body again. I even got a panic attack from it.

"Now, it has been suggested I might have tried to astrally project or something but I have never had anything like this happen to me. I never even tried to astrally project. So I had a panic attack. My body hurt. I felt tired and clouded. I went to lay down and fell asleep. Now that day, I had made up my mind I might have an attachment, as you said. So when I woke up I was still weak, could barely walk. I sat down and started saying what you told me over and over and over. About 'this is my body, I claim it' over and over. At night I said 'this is it. Either I die or you move on.' And I fell asleep saying this prayer over and over...

"Well, at I don't know what time, I remember waking up. I felt something or someone. So I said it over and over again. Finally I see what are like 4 or 5 shiny orb- like balls of light coming out of my body and all going into what looks like an envelope. The envelope seals and immediately I feel refreshed. I feel like myself. I knew something had happened and wanted to let you know.

"I tried to go back to sleep but couldn't. I was sooo energized. It was incredible. Around 2:15 am, I was ready to get up and start my day. I tossed and turned all night. My poor husband complained he couldn't sleep. That morning I woke up so refreshed, my husband thought I was crazy. He said he thought I would soon crash and burn. So yesterday I cleaned my house, the majority of it. I still had energy left over. In the night my tendonitis acted up, but that was it. No added tiredness or pain anywhere. My husband is amazed at the change. Today I woke up early again. Feel great. Not tired or anything. I just want to thank you from the bottom of my heart. You don't know how wonderful I feel. I haven't felt this healthy and strong in over 4 years. Thank you again!"

It is testimonials like this one that keep me going when I become frightened of exposing my knowledge to the world. I KNOW spirit attachment is a common affliction that is going completely unnoticed. It may not be a popular revelation, because think how many doctor appointments, procedures and prescriptions will be canceled once people realize they can heal themselves of all kinds of afflictions, conditions and symptoms. Your good health is NOT what the medical and pharmaceutical industries want. She emailed again a few days later.

"Hi there, I thought I would update you a bit. My husband just brought something to my attention. We contemplated it, and it corresponds to the time of me claiming my space. For the longest time, I was always cold. Felt cold to the touch, was cold. Super cold. My husband used to joke and say I was frigid cold, almost cadaver cold. Well right now he tucked his feet under my blanket and said "Ooh, nice and warm", and I realized, I have been warm. He has commented over and over on how warm I am now to the touch. So much so, that when he holds me I start to sweat. Go figure. We thought back and when I started to feel warm instead of cold and it's since I did my claiming of body. So thought I would share with you and see if this makes sense to you."

౪

These are only a few examples, but they contain many of the red flags one needs to look out for. I am hoping by sharing these situations with you, you will become familiar with the presentation of spirit attachment, and begin to recognize it when you see it. Often the symptoms can be very subtle. A person might say something odd, and it can be overlooked. Sometimes, if people are behaving oddly enough, they get diagnosed as mentally ill. I hope after reading this, you will consider there may be a perfectly logical explanation for that person's odd speech and behavior. And there's a perfectly simple and effective cure.

Sudden Death and Other Situations

I have become adept at recognizing red flags in conversation due to the benefit of my experience. It is my hope readers of this book will also develop an awareness of another level of activity taking place in their lives. Our teacher Leslie Temple-Thurston used to call it "the second attention." If you do your spiritual practice – grounding your energies, meditating, praying, etc, you eventually become aware of situations occurring underneath the obvious, conscious level. You may first become aware of the "second attention" with family. A person may say something, but you can tell there's more to the story, or there's an expression on their face belying the words that just came out of their mouth.

As your spiritual development deepens, you also learn that for every conscious fear and desire there is an equal and opposite unconscious desire and fear. So, part of the second attention is recognizing that the opposite of everything is true. Having this knowledge is particularly helpful when trying to determine whether spirit attachment is an issue. Some have referred to me as psychic, because I seem to have piercing intuition, but I think it is more likely I have a well developed ability to perceive the second attention. What's important to know is, if you know of someone who has died suddenly or been around others who have died suddenly, look carefully at survivors. Look for exaggerated grief or other emotion, suicidal feelings, or other feelings that don't seem to add up. If it seems like things don't add up, you probably have more (spirits of people) in the equation than are readily noticeable. Follow your instincts, and refer to the questionnaire in this book if you suspect spirit attachment (see Chapter 11). There are solutions, there is help. All you need is information that has been, until now, shrouded in mystery.

༄

Sudden Death

A young woman made a posting on my blog.

"My mother died suddenly 5 years ago. She woke up at half past five in the morning, went to the bathroom and, as she walked back to bed, fell down dead. It was later discovered she died of DVT. Since she died, there has been a lot of activity in the house. I always try to work out the logical before jumping to conclusions, but my sisters and father, who don't really know anything about the paranormal, have been noticing things happen too, like my mother's scent. On one occasion, we were all sitting in the living room reading and we all thought we heard something, but didn't tell each other, and later discovered we all thought we heard our mother calling. My father has seen flashing light in the living room and even went to the eye doctor so see if there was a problem with his eyes.

"The other week I woke up to the bedroom door opening. Things have gone missing and end up back where they were days later. My mother was always a bit of a prankster, and did that sort of stuff when she was alive, especially when it comes to the kitchen since she was a chef. Photos have been falling off the wall. **I personally think it is my mother trying to get our attention** and lately I have been sitting in the living room talking to her as if she is there, in the hope she is listening. My family have heard me talking "to myself" and think I have gone a bit weird, but I get some satisfaction in knowing she is there. **My problem is I am being told to let go and help her move on, and I don't want her to go. Is this selfish of me?"**

I replied, "It sounds like you're sure your mother has not passed on. What is DVT? I know you said you don't want to send her. When a person dies suddenly, they often don't even realize they're dead. And when it's a family member, they might be reluctant to go, even after they have figured it out. You can help her get to the Light, which is where she needs to go. It's very important for you and your family that your mother does not linger in her present form. **You can get her symptoms** and it can actually be harmful to you in other ways. **She has no idea she may be posing a health threat to you**. And when she goes into the Light, it doesn't mean your connection with her will be broken. You will always have a Love connection. And she will be there for all of you when it's your turn."

"I have several techniques that apply to your situation. There are several in my blog called, **What To Do if You Think You're Being Haunted (see chapter 11).** I offer specific instructions on what to do. If you can get your Dad and sisters to agree she may not have crossed over, you should all sit together and do the Space Claiming ceremony together. One or all of you will need to speak out loud, directly to her. Since she died suddenly, it will be an opportunity for any of you to tell her things you never had a chance to say. And someone will need to tell her she died that night. Let her know she is inadvertently affecting you and all who come into your home, and that you know she wouldn't want to be doing that. After you have all said any necessary apologies, forgivenesses and goodbyes, tell her to look for the Light. I'm sure she can see it. Tell her someone is there in the Light waiting for her."

"I understand the pain, believe me. I lost my brother when I was 11, my father when I was 18, and my mother when I was 20. It will be an emotional experience, but it is absolutely the right thing to do. It's better for your mother, so she can move on and do whatever is next in her destiny. You never know, she may come back as someone's baby! But it can't happen if she doesn't cross over."

"Please feel free to email me for any reason..."

"Hello there, thank you very much for your very informative message, a lot of stuff you mentioned makes complete sense. You asked what DVT is. It is Deep Vein Thrombosis, which causes a blood clot in the deep veins in the legs, except my mum got it from being asleep in bed. **You said something about getting the symptoms. Do you mean I could actually get the symptoms of what she died with? Because the other day I was rushed into Hospital with a DVT in my leg and, luckily, I had my blood thinned before anything else happened. But I was so scared because I actually thought, 'OMG I could die any minute if this clot moves' and all I could think about was how my mum died.**"

"Yes, if she attaches herself to you, you can have her symptoms, and it can be harmful, if not fatal, to you. But the good news is if you do the simple ceremony and say goodbye to her, her symptoms will go away with her. It's urgent. Please do my **Claim Your Space exercise** right away. Sudden death is a very confusing and painful thing for all concerned. But you can see now it's time for the next step. Aside from the emotional aspect, it's not a difficult process."

ଓ

Death of a Loved One

Dealing with the death of a loved one must be one of the worst human experiences. The sense of loss is too profound for words. There's the terror of being left alone, of feeling no one living can love you the way your deceased loved one did. Permanent separation from our loved ones brings up our deepest unconscious issue. My Corelight teacher says it's the very first split. Since the default experience of being human is duality (day/night, male/female, etc), we must begin somewhere. Our first human experience when we are born is feeling separated from God. When we are in the Oneness, we feel merged with everyone and everything, and we have the knowledge that there is no separation. I have concluded part of the human experience is to forget where we came from, once we are born. So, in essence, we are all programmed with an abandonment issue. It feels like God abandoned us. And the feeling is even more pronounced for those who are not cherished in their childhoods. When we follow a spiritual path, I believe it is due to our memory of and desire to merge once again with the Divine.

When a loved one dies, there is a strong desire to hold them here. The average person feels a deep sense of yearning, wishing the loved one could be here for a number of reasons. What the average person doesn't know is, our yearning can actually keep a loved one from deciding to cross over.

This message came one day.

"My mother died of pancreas cancer and I was there when she passed. She went very peaceful. She needed to go. She had suffered enough and had been sick for a long time. It hurt me to see her suffer the way she did. She was the only one left in my family who truly cared. The rest of my family members are very abusive to me for no reason, so I just ask others to help me through the grief. Just wish she knew how much I loved her."

I replied, "I can feel how much you are suffering. I'm thinking because everyone in your family is so abusive, your mother may have decided to stay behind and take care of you. But what she doesn't realize is her energy being mixed with yours is causing your suffering to be continuous. I believe the feelings you think are yours, are really hers. It's your feelings in reverse. It is her wondering if YOU know how much she loved YOU.

"If she is in your personal space, you will at some point take on her symptoms. It's very important you do a private ceremony, in your home or wherever you are comfortable, and talk to her. I believe she hears every word you say, because she has not crossed over. You need to tell her how much you love her. You need to tell her you know she loved you too. And you need to tell her she needs to look for the Light, and that someone she knows is there waiting for her. Tell her she can come back and visit you, but only after she has gone all the way into the Light.

"Your endless grief is an indicator she is in your space, and that is not the correct place for her to be."

"It's very funny you should say that because I was hurting in the right side of my stomach yesterday really bad. I just talked to my mother and told her I know she loved me and she cared for me, but she needs to go on to the Light and to be with the lord and I will be ok. I'm crying really bad right now. **The pain is horrible,** but she needs to be at peace. She suffered long enough. I will see her again. I know I will. She was a very strong woman and she loved me a lot."

"I forgot to say that you should say the Claim Your Space™ exercise out loud."

"Well she must know that I claim my own space and she has to go on to be with the Lord. I will be ok. It is still normal for me to grieve though, isn't it? I mean, she was my best friend."

"Absolutely normal to grieve. It's only been a few months. Give yourself until next August for full on grieving. My mother was my best friend, too. Let me know when the pain in your side goes away, okay?"

"What's weird about the pain is, my mom hurt there too before she died - several weeks before she died. Is that not weird?"

I stepped away from my email for a few hours and when I returned, I found she had sent me the same message twice. See below.

"DID YOU GET MY LAST MESSAGE? AND CAN YOU GIVE ME SOME KIND OF ANSWER? THANKS"

I tried to calm her, "Please understand if you are having a lot of fear right now, it may not be your feelings. Your mother is aware of our conversation and may be afraid for some reason to go to the Light. Your feelings and her feelings are intermingled now. Have you looked at my exercises yet? Just take your time. It's been four months now. You can take a day or so if you want. Talk to her. Say everything you need to say. Think of anything she might have needed to tell you, that she didn't. She's hanging on for some reason.

"Your explanation about everyone else being abusive is probably the main reason she has stayed with you. You can thank her for that. If there's anything she felt guilty about, forgive her (out loud). Tell her she is free now. She no longer has a body. But if she remains attached to you, she will make you sick, and I know she wouldn't want to do that.

"Also, ask her if there are any other spirits attached to you, and could she please take them with her to the Light. If you had an abusive childhood, it's possible you may have other spirits attached to you, and that may be one reason she doesn't want to leave.

"Ask your Guardian Angels to remove any earthbound spirits from your space and guide them to the Light. If you want, you can tell your mother she can wait until the others go, but she needs to go soon, because you are in pain. I know it sounds like a lot, but you can do this. You are Claiming Your Space as your own. Any other person, spirit, entity or energy form does not have permission to be in your space and needs to go now."

She replied, "No problem. I can do that and there is no fear, only me wishing she and I were still together. But I know it is not good for either one of us, and she needs to go to the Light. And yes, she needs to take whoever else is attached to me with her to the Light. I will be ok. God has always been there for me, which is why I have gotten this far my friend. Much love and God bless."

Sudden death is a situation that often leads to spirit attachment because the spirit is confused, and perhaps not even sure it is dead. It attempts to communicate with, hug, or talk to living loved ones. And when a survivor first hears of the loved one's death, that person is very vulnerable. Grief and the shattering of the psyche are an unfortunate combination. When people are grieving, friends and loved ones tend to ignore ominous or odd statements. People think, he's out of his head with grief. People think, she inherited the same disease her mother had. But it's more than that. The time immediately following the sudden death of a loved one is a very important time to make notes and pay attention to what a grieving person is thinking, saying and doing. You may well save that person's life, if you identify he is suffering from spirit attachment.

ೆ

Sexual Trauma and Blocked Chakras

I'm including this to elucidate that you can be hosting fragments of trauma and other people's energy without actually having a spirit attached to you. Here are excerpts from a blog exchange.

She started with, "I was reading your blog post about guiding spirits to the light and protecting oneself. I'm always so impressed with your gentle nature and how informative you are. I'd really like to learn more from you. Do you have experience with auras?"

I said, "A little bit. Why do you ask?"

"Oh, a "psychic" told me because of something very bad that happened to me long ago, my aura became completely closed. She said it's invisible and it can make people react badly to me. She wanted to charge me $600.00 to heal it, and I figured if she was really psychic, she would know I couldn't afford that."

I don't know if she was testing me, or if she didn't want to divulge more details, but it was clear she wanted guidance. So, based on the intuitive feelings I got from reading the message, I answered her.

"If it's something you know about, you can pray specifically to heal it. Sometimes trauma happens to us in this life because there's already an imprint in area from a past life event. A lot of people have suffered past life trauma, and it certainly can affect you in the here and now. In Buddhism, one of the prayers is to find the "inner magnet" that attracts certain people and circumstances to you, and dissolve it. You would do this with intention, and by monitoring your thoughts, words and deeds on a daily basis, to make sure you are not generating further negative karma for yourself. (See Chapter 12).

"You can do a lot with prayer. You can talk to your Higher Self or the Universe, or Spirit or God, or whatever works for you, and say if there IS a problem, please fix it. And give thanks knowing it is done. This is very powerful. There is nothing more powerful on this earth than your own intention.

"I know sometimes we close our chakras at certain areas for certain reasons, and that it can lead to illness. Usually trauma is the number one reason we shut down.

"So, say for example you had a sexual trauma. Perhaps you may have closed your second chakra, which is the chakra about two inches below the belly button, right where a woman's reproductive organs are. Or perhaps the opposite is true, and it is too open, or someone has "corded" you, continuing the abuse on a psychic level.

"The trauma itself might tend to repeat, so you may attract partners or relationships that tend to try to violate you. That may be what the psychic meant. Trauma is like a skip in a record. Similar events can happen over and over until it is cleared.

"Trauma can be like a vicious cycle until it is healed. If, for the sake of example, you were to sit quietly and think about your light body (chakras and aura) and focus on your second chakra, you could ask your guardian angels to make sure it is open appropriately for your greater good. Also ask that any cords be severed and any holes in your aura be repaired. You can do this with every chakra.

"The most important thing, though, is to consciously intend to open the crown chakra at the top of your head. That lets in the light that can heal everything, and make stuck issues begin to dissolve.

"If this bad thing happened to you in this life, and you are still mad at someone, or haven't forgiven someone, it is very important for your own healing to do your best to let go of this person completely in your heart and mind. If you carry rage or desire for revenge, those feelings can also act like a magnet, bringing further pain into your life.

"It sounds weird, but if you hold something against someone, right or wrong, it continues the relationship. So, maybe you should do my Claim Your Space exercise and kick out any energies that are not yours. In your case it might not be a ghost, but the remaining energy of someone who hurt you. You can evict it, and claim all of your energy as your own. You can also call back any energy you may have directed at this person, and take it back and bring your energy back into your own light body through the top of your head. You can call back your energy from any person or unpleasant situation that has ever upset or hurt or angered you.

"You don't need anyone's permission to take control of your space. It's yours and no one else's. You can use your own healing angels and repair any damage. It's kind of like a big game of pretend, but it really works.

"Sorry, I went on WAY too long. I hope I'm not off base. Feel free to ask any questions."

Her response took me by surprise, "Oh, Kelly, you're amazing! No, you didn't go on too long at all -- I was transfixed by every word.

"The past life and karma thing, when you mentioned it, it really struck me. The psychic said she had seen people who carried negative karma from past lives and when bad things happened to them in *this* life, it was because of that karma. She said in my case, I came into this life with extremely good, clean karma, and the "bad thing" (which was sexual assault -- your intuition was completely accurate) was never supposed to happen. She said I was not supposed to have it happen, and it was not supposed to be continuing to affect me. I lived my past lives so well, this life should have been free of these things.

"I haven't known what to do about this situation, because her words have haunted me but I didn't know where to turn or if I truly could believe what she was saying. It rang true, but when she asked for so much money and I'd even told her I'd lost my job, I wasn't really sure what to think.

"You've given me hope. I can't thank you enough for that. I can't thank you enough for taking the time to write such a thoughtful message to me. You make perfect sense -- my second chakra was ripped open when I was a child, and I think it was like a beacon to every predator whose path I crossed. I grew up thinking I was completely evil. I have never been able to come to terms with the fact that there were numerous incidents, unrelated to each other, in which I was violated, from the age of three and into my adulthood.

"And after reading the things here, I realize I've carried all of that with me. **And it has even led to physical illness in the form of severely painful endometriosis**. And I can feel terrible cords holding me to dangerous people. And you are so right -- I need to let all the rage go... because under my surface I am being eaten alive by a suppressed rage. And it's only hurting *me* instead of them. And if I hurt them, then I'm only damaging my own karma.

"I'm kind of blown away right now, sitting here stunned and letting it all sink in.

"You have done something so truly wonderful, Kelly. I'm sitting here with tears streaming down my face -- because all of this is just so incredible. I mean, how much longer would I have suffered with all of this if I hadn't reached out and opened up to you, a stranger on the internet? I'm going to study your blogs about grounding and shielding. I'm going to do everything you recommend. Kelly, thank you so much."

I said, "Don't guilt yourself about feeling rage. You certainly have every right to! It's just a very harmful energy, and it's bottled up inside you. I think Reiki can help dissolve some of your trauma and perhaps bring some relief for your endometriosis."

She replied, "I can't believe how lucky I am to have met you, a stranger on the internet. I'll be checking these things out -- you definitely have my curiosity, and I trust your guidance. Thank you so much for giving me this information. I'm very eager to finally heal, and you're so good at putting things into understandable, easily digestible terms. This isn't the first time someone has strongly recommended Reiki to me, and this time I'm going to heed the advice and pursue it. There's no way it could be appearing all around me and not mean something very important. Sometimes I can be so thick-headed when the Universe is prodding me. Kelly, thank you again for everything!"

ଓଷ

Traumatic Density Leads to Disease

In a previous chapter I shared about my father inflicting pain on my mother by squeezing the pressure point under her lower jaw bone, and how twenty three years later, she developed a highly malignant tumor in the same spot. The manifestation caused her death. That is a perfect example of how a traumatic imprint in the human energy field, held in place by intense emotion, eventually manifests as physical disease. Imagine how she must have felt, lying there in front of her young children, being tortured and humiliated by her husband, the man to whom she had dedicated her life. Imagine the shame, the feelings of betrayal, of powerlessness. And then over the years, as she struggled to raise five children by herself, imagine the intense feelings of abandonment and resentment. The abandonment patterning had been initiated in her childhood, and probably contributed to her reluctance to leave her abusive husband. Those intense emotions held the traumatic density in place, and aggravated the initial trauma site until eventually, she developed terminal cancer.

Even though she tried alternative treatment in the form of vegetable juice therapy to support the radiation treatment, it wasn't enough to overcome the root issues. On her deathbed, my mother tearfully admitted that she had truly been in love with my father. She said, after his terrible tirades, he would cry like a child and beg her forgiveness, and say he couldn't live without her. So she would forgive him. She couldn't reconcile it, having been gullible enough to love a man who became so utterly evil and abusive. According to her upbringing, a "good" wife never leaves her husband. But by staying as long as she did and cleaving to her husband like a good Catholic, she allowed terrible years of abuse to be inflicted upon her children, the children put in her care by God, the children she adored. She felt defeated, responsible for the death of my brother, and the damage done to all of them. The emotion of shame, failure and a broken heart fueled the cancer until it overtook her entire body and claimed her life.

If she had known about energetic clearing, the outcome might have been different. This is what I am saying. Even in the face of such overwhelming patterning and experience, sincere efforts to claim one's space can turn around situations such as this. It might have allowed her to forgive herself and my father and experience some joy in her life before she left the planet. Hypothetically, if she had known about energetic clearing and had begun it immediately after my father left, it might indeed have been the thing to heal my brother's shattered heart and soul. She might have been able to clear her own energy field as well as her children's, and they all might have been able to heal and thrive. But they didn't know how... This spiritual solution was never taught to them.

We are delicate webs of energy, and we are entitled to be in control of our energy bodies. You just need to know what to look for, and then take the simple steps to reclaim your personal space, doing exercises to familiarize yourself with your energy bodies, and intending for your own perfect healing. The important thing to remember is, emotion is the glue that keeps the traumatic density in place. You really need to figure out the initial emotion. It's not hard. You can look at any current issue, break it down and determine what the polarity is. Is it victim/tyrant? Is it cherished/abandoned? What makes you angry or upset? Since we continuously repeat our patterning, the issue in your life right now will have the same components as the root issue, the first traumatic incident that set your imbalance in place. You have all the clues.

If you do the grounding exercise, spending a few minutes per day focusing inward, you will recognize discomfort or suddenly remember something, the answer will come. If you can't figure it out, simply acknowledge during your prayers that you recognize you are in a pattern and you want to be free of it. The key is that you bring to conscious awareness your realization of being locked in a pattern of thoughts, words, and perhaps deeds, and you express your intention to clear the ingrained pattern that is making you ill. When victimization is an issue, the recapitulation exercise is particularly effective (see Chapter 11).

You can start with the tools outlined in this book, and expand to further forms of meditation, healthy diet, hypnotherapy, yoga, singing, whatever you feel will aid you in your determination to become completely familiar with *you*, inside and out.

You're not crazy

"Humanity is surrounded by the thought influence of millions of discarnate beings, who have not yet arrived at a full realization of life's higher purposes. A recognition of this fact accounts for a great portion of unbidden thoughts, emotions, strange forebodings, gloomy moods, irritabilities, unreasonable impulses, irrational outbursts of temper, uncontrollable infatuations and countless other mental vagaries."

Dr Carl Wickland, <u>Thirty Years Among the Dead</u>. 1930

One of Patty's specialties was being able to detect densities in people's human energy fields. Often the densities were the spirits of people who had died, but had somehow not gone to the Light. Together, we made contact with these spirits, gave them an opportunity to communicate with their host and eventually sent the spirits to the Light. We helped many people free themselves from the hell of being attached by a symptomatic ghost or spirit that was making them sick. Our results qualify as miracles as far as I'm concerned, in that people with debilitating and life-threatening symptoms were restored to normal in the course of a session or two, and trapped spirits were enabled to go on with their appropriate next step, which was to go to the Light.

During that period, I became well versed in many aspects of spirit depossession, and am writing this book in order to utilize my experience for the good of as many people as possible.

When you have a spirit attached to you, it can feel like you're losing your mind. In actuality, you are sharing your mind. If you're lucky, the change is so sudden and dramatic, it is undeniable. You can hear a voice in your head you never heard before, or you suddenly crave tobacco or drinks you never craved before. But often, you can carry the spirit of a person for so long, boundaries are long blurred, and you don't know where your thoughts end and someone else's begin. Or, you pick up the spirit in a moment of vulnerability, such as while under anesthesia, during a trauma, or while intoxicated, and reality is somewhat skewed anyway. As you begin to recover from whatever it was, you find that somehow, you're different. And you learn to adapt, rather than question.

The situation is complicated, too, by the fact that you are feeling someone else's feelings. One minute you can know something is wrong, and the next minute you are rationalizing everything that has been happening. Because you are emotionally, mentally and physically linked with the attached spirit, perspective is easily lost. And if alcohol, drugs or mental illness are prominent in your life, the situation can go unnoticed for quite a while. Often drugs, alcohol or a pre-existing condition are seen as the causes of the new and unusual behavior.

You can go to medical facilities in search of a cure. But the cure is not to be found there. You may be suffering from a heart palpitation, yet the test results are normal. You may feel sure you are pregnant, yet the test comes back negative. You can swear you don't recall saying or doing the thing you have been accused of. You may desperately plead with your doctor, only to be referred to a psychiatrist, or put on some antidepressant, to 'see' how it goes. And your symptoms still don't go away.

This is an energetic problem, and an energetic solution is needed to help you free yourself from the bind. It is difficult for the practitioner, because it requires trust to begin the healing. The afflicted person needs to, in a moment of clarity, agree to accept help in being freed from this 'other.' Even if a person agrees, he or she may become filled with fear and try to back out before the actual healing takes place. You see, once we have a dialogue about claiming your space, the attached spirit knows you are going to try to send it away, and it can become afraid. It then begins to have doubt and panic, which the host perceives as his or her own feelings.

I can see how the realization of this problem could have led to, in the past and in some third world cultures to this day, the so-called possessed being tied down, coerced and subjected to various forms of deprivation and abuse. The pages of Catholic history are filled with tragic examples. On a cellular level, there is the collective memory of the mass murders called Inquisitions that took place in centuries past, when women and others were accused of being witches or being possessed by or in league with the Devil, were tried by torture and horribly killed. So, when we begin to discuss the situation, the afflicted often has a double whammy – her ingrained fears and the fears belonging to the attached spirit.

Our approach was different, in my opinion, from a typical exorcist because, for us, it was all about compassion- for the host and the spirit. We came from the understanding that we are all one. There is no "other," really. There is no "evil." We are all one. The attached spirit is a spiritual being, a former human being, who somehow got lost or confused or bound to the earth plane by guilt, confusion or trauma. Even if the attached spirit was someone who committed murder, rape or other heinous crimes in his life, he was still stuck in limbo and needed our assistance. It was not our place to judge. We simply acknowledged the presence of the being, explained that it somehow lost its way, and offered an opportunity for it to take its next appropriate step. Often, the spirit was someone who felt the need to apologize to the host for past wrong doing, and after we gave the spirit the opportunity to do that, it would feel okay about moving on.

We never encountered anything remotely demonic, and our compassion for both host and spirit seemed like a completely unique approach. Ghosts are people too. Unfortunately, nowadays, investigators are calling themselves ghost hunters and ghost chasers, as if the ghosts are bad. I believe this attitude only makes things worse. How would you like to be hunted or chased? The whole situation of spirit possession is a deeply spiritual issue. Both parties are afflicted and need help. There really is no need to turn one party into "the Good guy" and one into "the Bad guy." Unconditional love is what heals the situation. Just because the possessing individuals are physically invisible, they are still beings of God. They are stuck as a result of some physical or emotional trauma, and deserve as much compassion and care as we can offer.

Even though I established that we are not talking about demons and devils, I thought the other day, if God created everything, how can one say that he didn't create demons? And who was Lucifer before he "fell"? He was the top angel, at the right hand of God. Good and Evil must have been one of the first polarities to be put in place, along with Self/Other and Male/Female. Those three polarities are among the first "splits" human kind experienced as a set up for life on earth. Self/Other was the split from God into human form. The Male/Female polarity was highlighted by the Adam and Eve story and Good/Evil by the fruit of the tree of knowledge and the serpent who spoke to Eve. If so much of the Bible is filled with allegory and parables, why do some people take these parts, about Adam and Eve and the origin of Evil, so literally? It was the establishment of our default setting. They are examples of the main polarities we have to deal with daily.

Patty rarely expressed fear of the energies we encountered, although some of the images and life events she witnessed were breathtaking. No matter how frightening the characters appeared, she treated each spirit with the same compassion. She was too spiritually evolved to get caught up in the "Good/Evil" polarity. If all the problems were being caused by the energies of the deceased, whether they had been "bad" in life or not, our job was to help them move on. Our priority was always to identify and remove the source of the emotional charge that kept the "haunting" in place. It was most definitely not our place to judge, and judging would have been counterproductive anyway, because a spirit who feels judged will continue to be angry and resentful, and will not willingly move on. And that would be bad for our client, and the spirit.

ଓ

After helping depossess people for all those years, I have concluded that personal intention is just about the most powerful force on earth, and a person can, by her own intentions and interactions with the Divine, free herself. Even with helpers, the key to the process is for the afflicted person to state out loud her intention to have her space as her own. But if a person cannot get beyond the mindset of the attached spirit, or beyond her own limitations of trust due to childhood abuse or what have you, she may remain afflicted, in effect, choosing to share her space with someone who does not belong in her body. I had a sad example like this happen a few years ago. Here are excerpts from her rambling emails. On one hand, she was reaching out for help, but on the other, she couldn't trust me enough to accept it. She was defying medical science and all rational explanations, yet refused our service, which would have finally and non-invasively solved her problem. I don't know what ever happened to this woman. See the ambivalence on many levels.

"Things are happening to me that have not happened before. Right now, I am getting impressions that I am pregnant, and yes, I've been pregnant twice before and I know what that feels like...

"The catch is, I am 46 years old and my two sons are grown and in college. Yes, I am feeling that empty nest type feeling, though was aware and ready to deal with it. I went to the cemetery by chance one day, as I sometimes like wandering and looking at people's names. I like to wonder about what types of people these individuals were. Many times I believe I have said a spiritual "hello" and communicated through my inner thoughts and voice.

"Later, or earlier (I do not recall now), I started to get these inner sensations - like a kick. I also had an image of a girl with long blonde hair when I woke up one day. Then I had a dream about a tired and bored mother. The next morning I thought it meant I should be taking Folic Acid! I've been taking it ever since. Why would I think that?

"At first I thought, 'I'm pregnant.' I went to see a doctor and a specialist. The doctor said there is nothing to report, and the fertility specialist actually got the camera out and showed me that I was not pregnant, almost indignantly and annoyed! I truly believed I was pregnant. I even went to a psychic institute and the men who read me said I wasn't pregnant either! I was so adamant, based on the feelings I was having, that I thought it must have been a mistake, and that technology must be so far advanced that I was impregnated by cellular cloning, or I may have been injected by something! I was a crash test dummy, a guinea pig, or something. I was convinced and I'm still not too sure, yet it seems so out there as I am speaking of it. I am lost, frustrated and becoming depressed.

"I once said out loud, if I could just get through training to become a psychic then I would save all the children I could from sexual abuse, as I believe it is becoming more rampant and being interwoven in our society at an incredible speed, yet the crimes are so unspoken. While I was being sexually abused by a neighbor, I escaped through a trap door in my mind and went traveling over the fields, and on and on. When I think of these things happening to another child, this makes me want to cry. Every time I think of a child being hurt by sexual abuse, it shakes my very soul. I am so saddened that I feel helpless at this point in my life, as I have no money to get by and I am in an unhappy relationship. I think I may have picked up a little child, to either keep me happy in my empty nest, or perhaps this child was empathetic to my sorrows? Perhaps this is how the child died - he was one year old approximately at death. I don't know, I just know the feelings of pregnancy are stronger every day. Can you help me?"

I responded immediately, offering her solutions she could begin using right away, like the hot salt bath, and the Claim Your Space exercise. I explained what I thought was happening to her, and reassured her that whatever we found in her space would be sent appropriately to the Light.

She responded, "Thank you so much for responding so quickly. I do know my own answers, yet this one I am a bit baffled by... and it has not cleared up despite the many healings I have had already. If you would like to try it, I would be honored to try anything."

I thought she would call soon, but more time went by, and she didn't commit to an appointment. So I emailed her, encouraging her to come and have a healing. I am normally not so persistent, but her symptoms seemed so obvious, I felt sure we could offer her relief. In hindsight, I realized that my persistence may have exacerbated her doubt, and I will never take the persistent approach again.

"Hello Kelly, I feel like I'm emailing Ghostbusters! Yes, I did the bath with salt, and let the possible being know that I would like my space back and to go to the light. I've asked several times and have also used my Supreme Being to help, though nothing is working. Interestingly, the lights in the bedroom went off and on a few times, the television was making unusual noises and the microwave and coffeemaker went out - they don't work anymore! So either it's a coincidence, or not!

"Amazingly enough, my body is also changing like I am pregnant. The movements are so real, it is hard to believe it may be anything else. I might be holding onto my wish that

I'm pregnant and thinking it's some sort of miracle - we can't send away a real life can we? What if it is true that I am holding a child and the doctors are wrong? Alot of unusual things happen to me. So nothing is impossible, right?

"Reasonable or not, I do need to make an appointment with you and ask you what the next step is. I don't know what to do and I know I need to ask myself and I should know my own answers, yet I'm very confused right now. I'm not really afraid. In fact, I've been getting a clairaudient message too, "I want my mommy", and a constant ringing-like sound. What do I do with that? The baby's headstone said it was about a year old. I also ask myself if I'm supposed to figure this out, or if this is a spirit lost?"

I was concerned by her words – "asking the possible being", saying she "would like" her space back. I felt due to her early childhood abuse, she didn't really know how to be in control of her own energy field. Her boundaries had been blurred and violated at a very young age.

I felt the spirits of a pregnant mother and her young child or children were possessing our client. They had probably died around the same time, of some kind of fever, and were buried in the same cemetery. The pregnant mother and young child were still yearning for each other after death. Their feelings of separation from each other may have reflected their circumstance at the time of death – most folks isolate someone with an infectious disease - and also perhaps matched her "empty nest" feelings. Our potential client's protective feelings were not even hers, she was sharing her thoughts and feelings with her "company", and their fears translated into her becoming doubtful of me. With her next response, I knew we had lost her.

"Okay, I'll call and make an appointment soon, or perhaps I may change my mind. I believe there are two things going on. I am carrying a child (my dreams - a boy with brown hair or a girl with blonde hair), and two, I did take a small spirit essence with me from the gravesite and it is trying to communicate with me. The reason I'm getting the clairaudience is because I think someone is going to take this child away from me. This child within will be like my son who disliked being away from me as a child, and called for his "mommy" often. Someone is going to try to take this child away from me. This is my feeling."

Notice how she said twice that someone was going to take the child from her? That is an example of the host experiencing the fears of the spirit. Those were not necessarily her feelings. I continued to theorize that a pregnant woman and her children had died for some reason. Perhaps they had succumbed to a fever. Perhaps if the woman caught a fever, she was kept from her infant son, and they were both consumed with separation anxiety. The mother's spirit may have stayed behind out of concern for her infant son and perhaps other children, and they all remained in the cemetery. When this compassionate, lonely, modern-day woman came along, the spirit of the pregnant mother, who was still looking for her infant son, possessed her. Our client began to feel the symptoms of pregnancy, the anxiety of separation, their predominant emotions at the time of death. And the suspicion of intent to separate them was being projected onto me, as the depossessor. She was swayed by the emotions of the spirits.

She was initially vulnerable for some reason, probably because of the fracturing caused by the early childhood sexual abuse and her admitted empty-nest emotional state, and she was perfectly willing to assume the role of mother. She was even willing to refute medical evidence, and believed with all her heart that she was pregnant. Because she had been invaded against her will when she was a vulnerable child, she was afraid to trust the practitioners, even as she allowed the spirits to invade her and stay in her space. And she chose not to show up for a healing.

ಌ

I have another example, of a young woman whose health was already compromised before her supernatural events began. She was being tormented with audial hallucinations in her room. It turned out that she had the spirit of a friend attached to her. But because of some misleading information she got from a psychic, she hadn't figured it out.

"Sorry to bother you. But the noises are getting worse in my room. As I was falling asleep, my radio started making this noise, turning on slowly by itself. But I didn't see anyone and I yelled, "STOP" and I turned on the light to see what was going on and I fixed my radio. And then the banging noises on my wall started to get REALLY loud and I started to hear my spirit guide talk, but I was too scared to hear what she said because of what just happened and I tried to ignore it. Then I heard this female scream so loud that it woke me up, I think it was my spirit guide trying to wake me up to see if I was okay since I wasn't feeling good and I woke up scared and I ran to my sister's room and I asked her if it was her that screamed and she told me "No." I really don't know what is going in my room but it needs to stop. And right before I woke up this morning, my radio started to make that noise again but I ignored it. What should I do?"

Notice how she referred to a 'spirit guide' and that it was a 'she.' Out of curiosity, I read her blog page, only to find a posting about a friend of hers who had died. The odd thing was, it wasn't a recent death, and therefore unusual that this person would still be mourning the loss of her friend so intensely. It piqued my investigative curiosity. Here is how I responded to her.

"I just read your blog about your friend who died 6 years ago. PLEASE consider that your friend Ashley is the one who is screaming in your ear and banging on your walls. She needs to be sent to the light. Please email me and tell me how she died... We should talk about this... Don't be alarmed, it's all beginning to make sense."

"She had heart problems and heart surgery when she was younger, and all of these other surgeries. Once we went into a pool at a hotel, and I could see all of these scars on Ashley's body and it made me really sad. She had a nurse with her in middle school in case something happened, and she had to take medication for her heart. I was the first person to become friends with her when she came into the school in the middle of 8th grade. She was Hispanic and she was so beautiful. My parents are Hispanic, so Ashley and I would talk to each other in Spanish all the time and she would thank me every day for being her friend.

"She was really skinny and I got worried because I didn't know at the time what was wrong with her. After school ended, I got a phone call from the lady who took care of her, telling me that Ashley was in the hospital since her heart got ill. Ah, I'm about to cry typing this, but I need to let it out. The nurse would call me every day to update me on her. She told me how she'd had surgery and how she was on the machine that keeps you alive. And 3 days later Ashley died.

"The day she died, I had to go out of town. I was scared that she was going to die and my Mom kept on telling not to think about it and be strong. Well when we got back, there were 4 messages on the answering machine, from the lady who took care of her and from my 3 friends and they were crying. I called the lady. She told me that Ashley had passed away and my heart just fell apart. I dropped the phone and ran into my room. I didn't go to her funeral because I was too depressed. I feel guilty that I didn't get the chance to say goodbye to her. I know I shouldn't feel guilty, but I do because I wished that I could have said goodbye to her, but I was too depressed. I'm glad she isn't suffering anymore. The only thing I have left of her is when she signed my yearbook. I hope she isn't mad at me since I didn't say goodbye to her. That's the story."

Here is my response to her. "When Ashley passed away, she may have come straight over to your house. It makes sense, since you were her best friend, and she didn't get to say goodbye. It's also possible that if she died during surgery, she may not know she's dead, even after all these years. It would also make sense that you still have such a hard time accepting her passing, because if she is still with you, you can FEEL her presence, and it's like constant torture. She of course would not want to be causing you suffering, and she needs to know that it is better for you and for her if she goes to the Light.

"Would you be willing to assume (or pretend) that Ashley IS with you? If yes, you can speak directly to her and say all the things you want to say. Explain to her that she died in the hospital. Apologize for not being there the day she died and tell her how much you miss her.

"You will need to tell her that as much as you love her, she really needs to move on to the Light, so that she can get a brand new healthy body and come back into a new life. Ask her to look around and see if there are any other spirits attached to you, or in your house, that she could take with her into the Light. Thank her for doing this.

"Then call on your Guardian Angels and Healing Angels, and Ashley's too, and ask them to help clear your space completely, and remove any entities who may not be able to move themselves.

"I hope you can find the courage to do this simple yet powerful exercise, and I'd love to hear if things settle down for you right away. You could even print this out and read it to her. Sending spirits to the Light is the most compassionate thing you can do, especially because they are in a state of confusion, and as long as they are, they are unable to take their next appropriate step in their own development. And they don't realize they are negatively affecting the living."

She replied, "I know Ashley is around me, I can feel her presence. It's very strong and very comforting. Every time I think about her, and I start to cry, this comforting feeling will come all over me like someone is hugging me and I'll suddenly stop crying. I know it's her, because I know she doesn't want me to cry over her. I met a Psychic and she is the one that told me about my two Spirit Guides and the Spirit named Charles that haunts my room. She hasn't been able to get through to

Ashley but she has been able to get through to this girl who met Ashley up in Heaven and are friends. You seem to be the only one to get through to her. Hearing what you said to me is what I've been looking for this whole entire time. I've been wondering so long if Ashley ever visits me and I got my question answered.

"I'm really glad I found you. Thank you very much for telling me all of this. I know how Spirits can hear you talk through your mind because I told one of my Spirit Guides 'Hello' and she said 'Hello' back, I heard it loud and clear. I do have the Courage and Strength to do this, I know it will be hard saying goodbye to her but I hope I will see her again one day.

"I told Ashley last night through my head to go into the light and I told her how much I loved her and how I miss her so much and how she is dead and confused. When I walked into my room before I told her this, it was so peaceful and quiet and I didn't hear any banging noises or voices, and I was able to sleep. When I told her to go into the light and into the tunnel I did hear a few noises like there was a lot of people walking on my carpet in my room and I heard her voice, but it was very faint, I couldn't hear what she said clearly but it sounded like she said 'Bye Marie.' The walking noises continued and I heard her bang on my wall and that was it. I was able to sleep for the rest of the night.

"Thank you SO much for everything. I feel a lot better now knowing what I have to do and who haunts my room, I'm not scared of Ashley at all. Yesterday after dinner I went to my room and I started to talk to her. I didn't speak through my head; I spoke to her out loud. It got really cold in my room when I was talking to her. I was freezing, but I wasn't scared. But I didn't hear her say anything or bang on the wall, it just got really cold in my room. Thank you once again for your help Kelly, I really appreciate it."

A few days later I heard from her again, "I just wanted to give you an update and tell you that I heard no noises last night in my room. I'm glad it's finally over."

I was really curious about her symptoms, so I finally asked her, "Did you ever tell me about your health problems?"

"Sometimes I'll have panic attacks and they will get pretty bad. I have a heart murmur and there is a mild leakage in one of the valves. I have Irritable Bowel Syndrome. I'm allergic to milk. I hate it when my stomach gets upset. I just wish I could feel good every day. Before I get my PMS my stomach will get really upset so it just really sucks that I have all of these problems. I just want to be healed and have it go away. Sometimes I feel like crying because of how bad my stomach will get and I end up shaking and losing weight.

"I want to thank you for everything. You have been such a big help. You have taught me a lot and you helped me send Ashley into the light. I know she's much happier now. You are probably right, since I have had 3 surgeries, and my heart appointments used to be at a hospital. So I definitely think that someone got attached to me. I hope I'll feel much better when this is all over. I think that a bad Spirit got attached to me to tell you the truth."

There were many red flags in her story. The obvious things were the panic attacks, banging on the wall, and the female voice screaming in her ear. She was thrown off the track when someone told her that was a spirit guide. Her friend was trying so hard to get her attention. The girl is clearly sensitive, feeling changes in temperature, and feeling the emotions of others. And the panic attacks are usually a sign of multiple spirits attached. When she said she heard the sound of many people walking on her carpet, I think she was witnessing the exit of multiple spirits. She probably did pick them up during her own surgeries and hospital visits. Because she said she still felt her room get very cold after doing the Claim Your Space™ exercise, I suspected she still had more clearing to do. A few weeks later she emailed again and said the banging on the wall was back... but she claimed her space again and it went away.

It's really amazing how often a person really does have all the pieces of the puzzle, but never puts them together. Here was this girl, posting 'help' messages on my blog, wondering what was happening to her. At the same time, she had posted an article about the friend she had lost six years prior. It was obvious to me that her friend's death and her bizarre experiences were connected. Because this young woman's immune system is compromised, she may continue to struggle with intermittent possessions. But at least she has tools to deal with it now, and doesn't have to wonder if she's crazy, or go get a prescription from the psychiatrist.

I had postulated that because of her pre-existing immune suppression, she might have ongoing problems with spirit attachment. I checked in on her every few weeks for several months. Once, I asked how things were going, and she informed me that her cat had just died. She explained how devastated she was, and how much she missed him.

"I hope he went to Cat heaven after he died. Today is the one month anniversary of his death. I am doing pretty well today. I just wish that he would come and visit me in spirit so I can hear or see him one last time."

I replied, "Haven't you had enough of being visited by spirits? You really need to stop asking for that! I hope you feel at peace very soon."

A few weeks later she responded.

"I'm so tired of it. I don't ask for it, it just happens. I keep hearing this creepy music noise in my room that lasts a few seconds. It has a beat to it and it scares the crap out of me. I want it to go away."

I answered, "For some reason, you are open to other realms."

A day later she said,

"I just wanted to let you know that last night I used your Protection Verse and Claiming Your Space. It really helped. I didn't experience anything at all, so I was able to sleep peacefully without being woken up."

Without further encouragement, the young woman used the tools I had already given her, and she claimed her space. It only took a minute, and her problem was solved. She didn't need to go running to her sister or mother and be put in the uncomfortable position of feeling like everyone thought she was crazy.

Case Study - Jeannie

Here is an example of someone dealing with what she perceived to be Evil. I want you to see how the process of realization and self-discovery works, by sharing this series of emails with you. This is how I am able to do this work "remotely." I worked with this person over a three month period until, finally, all the pieces fit, and she was successfully able to depossess herself. The necessary ingredient to begin is the intent to get to the root of your suffering once and for all. In this case, she had tried the medical route for a very long time.

Her initial email is a bit cryptic, but you can tell her childhood was horrendous. So, I had her do the questionnaire.

Date: Jan 8th, 10:43 PM

"I had a breakdown in 1998. Memories from the past caught up with me. Not only myself, but my whole family were victims. My brother's memories came back a year earlier, but until I called him and told him about mine, he never said anything. When my sister started getting memories, she literally withdrew into herself. Towards the end, she couldn't even talk. It was all jumbled. She couldn't face it. She died about a year later. We are the type of people who have to know for sure, so we started calling families and our memories were verified. My uncle was a very evil man. He hounded our family for years. I would have to write a book to tell the story. It's ironic that he died in church at the pulpit. The healing goes on for life."

Spirit Attachment Questionnaire

Do you suffer from anxiety or panic? *yes*

Have you been diagnosed with any psychiatric or mood disorders? *yes see above*

Do your moods change quickly for no apparent reason? *yes*

Are you or have you ever been suicidal? *no*

Do you know anyone who has committed suicide? *yes*

Do you REALLY, REALLY miss one of your deceased relatives or friends? *no*

Has a loved one died, and are you finding that you now have similar symptoms to the deceased? *no* (*But later she realized she was experiencing symptoms her mother had before she died*).

Have you been told that you have "inherited" a disease that someone else in your family has already died of? *no*

Do you have any chronic physical illnesses that won't go away, or that Doctors cannot seem to cure? *yes*

Do you have insomnia? *yes*

Do people ever say that you did or said something, but you have no recollection of doing or saying it? *no*

Has anyone ever said that you talk in your sleep? *no*

Do you ever "hear" voices, or thoughts in your head that don't seem like they're yours? thoughts, *yes*

Do you ever "see" or smell people or things that other people can't? *no*

Do you ever "feel" that you are not alone? *yes*

Over time, have you developed any addictions to food or alcohol or drugs that you didn't have before? *no*

Can you think back to the time when your habits changed? Did something happen around that time? *yes*

Have you ever engaged in self-destructive behavior – cutting your skin or hair, picking at your skin or face, battering yourself or other things? *no*

Did you suffer from early childhood abuse, whether physical, sexual or emotional? *yes*

Have you ever been under general anesthesia? How many times? List dates and reasons for the surgery. *Yes, tubal ligation in 1986 and hysterectomy in 1997.*

Have you ever lost a child, born or unborn? *Yes, 3* Have you ever toured a battlefield or place of extreme decimation of human life? (Gettysburg, Auschwitz, Hiroshima, etc?) *no*

Have you spent a period of time in any kind of medical facility? Hospital, convalescent home, treatment center? no Have you ever used drink or drugs to the point of blackout (walking and talking, but not remembering a period of time). *no*

Have you ever used drink or drugs to the point of unconsciousness? *no*

Does someone in your immediate family suffer from any of the above symptoms or experiences? *no*

"I took this quiz, because I do feel like someone is with me. I feel my parents and sister a lot, but not in the same way."

Based on the results of the questionnaire, I suggested she do the Claim Your Space™ exercise, bath, etc.

Date: Mar 8

"Dear Kelly,

"I followed your suggestion about clearing. As I have told you before, I have felt someone with me. I will let you know how the clearing went. I have had one problem after another over this last year, and my feeling is that my uncle has been around me. The medical people can't seem to find any answer to my problems. I do some energy healings, so I am familiar with what energy can do, so I have tried your energy and divine light exercise. I feel the problems are coming from around me. This may sound strange, but my uncle never could get my mind as a child and I am not so sure he has given up. He was truly evil. Even to the point of killing his own grandchild, and so many more. My problem might be that because of the trauma of it all, I can't let it go. There is still so much buried. I can handle what I know. It's the unknown that causes the problems. Well I could write a book about this, so I will leave it at this.

"This is just too strange Kelly. I went yesterday and had my esophagus stretched. It hasn't seemed to help. It was restricted and they want another go at it in three weeks. They say everything looks okay other than the restriction, but this just keeps on going and going. It's been a year and a half now. I've lost 40 pounds. Everyone tells me it's in my head, which doesn't help matters at all. Maybe it is in my head from something that happened as a child, but if I can't call it forward then I can't work with it. Any suggestions? I will keep on with the clearings. Sometimes I just want to give up, but then my stubbornness kicks in. It's been a long tough battle and that is just the way I feel about it. It is a battle.

"Thanks for your concern and help. Jeannie"

Date: Mar 9

"Jeannie,

"I know this may be unfathomable, but people like your uncle feel they cannot go to the Light because of what they have done, and need to feel that they are forgiven.

"If, in your meditative state, or by an intermediary, it could be made clear to him that he WILL be welcomed into the Light, and that that is where he will find forgiveness and peace, it may loosen his hold. I feel he is pretty sure he's not welcome in Heaven.

"And it sounds like forgiving him may be more than you are willing or able to do. Believe me, my father was wicked, too, and I'm sure it's impossible for some of my siblings to forgive him. But it is usually forgiveness and accepting apologies on behalf of these earthbound spirits that enables them to let go and leave you alone.

"When I worked in partnership with the psychic medium, we were often faced with people such as your uncle, and they were surprisingly desperate, and feeling stuck. But the game is over, it has been since the day he died, and he is prolonging his own agony by staying in this neitherworld.

"He needs to be convinced, in an impassive sort of way, that the most logical, practical and acceptable thing for him to do is decide to go into the Light. When he gets there, he will get an opportunity to take the next step in his own evolutionary process, whatever that may be.

"Usually you can outsmart abusers this way - by convincing them that they are putting themselves at a disadvantage in their current action. He might not let go for your benefit, but he might let go for his own.

"You may feel he doesn't deserve to go to heaven, but really, it's not up to us. He's dead now, and he needs to move on. Perhaps, if you are holding rage and blame against him, that might be the part that needs to be released. Does that make sense?

"The most important thing is for him to be gone from your space, even if it means you forgiving him or accepting an apology on his behalf...

"This technique has worked in the stickiest of situations.
"Do you have a meditative type friend who would sit with you and help you clear your uncle? I can help with a script and the grounding exercise, etc.

"Blessings,

Kelly"

Date: Mar 13

"Dear Kelly,

"The strange thing is, I have forgiven them all. I have the belief that whatever happens in our lives is for a reason and to learn. I would not be what I am today without ALL the experiences I have had. From the experience as a child, I developed some wonderful gifts. I had to laugh, because almost all of my friends are the meditative type. I was just visiting with one and telling her about you.

"The truth is, when I think about all that happened when I was a child I feel sorrow for them (abusers). I once had a psychic tell me there was someone who was jealous of me that was around causing me problems. I couldn't determine who that could be. Maybe with your help I can get this figured out. I actually had the energy to go for a walk today. I did a clearing the other night. Maybe it helped. Thanks Kelly.

Jeannie"

She's already noticing an improvement, and she thought of another aspect that needed to be cleared.

Date: Apr 2

"Hi Jeannie!

"How are you doing today? I'm guided to tell you that in your case, it might be completely appropriate to use the Claim Your Space™ exercises daily, and repeatedly.

"Did you read my testimonials about success stories? (see Chapter 7). One lady decided that spirit attachment was the cause of her symptoms, and she was relentless for a few days, saying the phrases over and over. She had some weird flare ups (typical), and luckily she pressed on. Many people are frightened by flare ups into stopping the clearing. She finally gave some kind of ultimatum by intent, and it worked. She saw 5 orbs leave her body, and her energy came back in a big rush.

Kelly"

Date: Apr 4

"Dear Kelly,

"I had to send you another message. I read the testimonials and 90% of them pointed their finger at me. When my mother died, she could not eat. We would try to feed her and she said she just couldn't. I went for 6 months barely able to eat anything. I admit that I feel guilt for not bringing her home with me because the circumstances around her death were suspicious. I wish I could talk to someone that understood all of this. I got verification from her that her life was taken. It's a story that spans over 60 years. I have just learned to keep quiet, because it is so unbelievable to most people. I carry all this with me, so it may not be a haunting, but a bomb that is exploding within. The counselor I went to several years ago was way too condescending. I would have probably ended up in a padded cell.:) I tend to be a logical person, but in some cases, logic as society defines it, just doesn't answer the questions."

She realized that her symptoms of the past 18 months were similar to her mother's deathbed symptoms, but still not totally ready to accept the idea of attachment.

Apr 8

"Jeannie,

"So, do you think your mother may have stayed with you after she passed, and that's why you couldn't eat? It could explain that intense guilt you felt, too. Do you think that you may have some of the same habits, moods or personality traits your mother used to have? If she's still attached to you, the emotions you are feeling could be intense, or conflicting, because they would be your feelings AND hers. If she realized, after her death, exactly what had happened to her, she could be in a rage, and not wanting to cross over until she sets things right. Or, might she have decided to stay, thinking she could protect you from someone or something?

"The problem with that, if she is attached to you, is that she is unwittingly causing you to suffer because you are experiencing all of her fears, symptoms and emotions. If you have any kind of desire to set things right on behalf of your mother, please consider that she may still be with you.

"If you'd like to tell the story of your mother's death, I would be happy to hear it. When you say her life was taken, what do you mean? It sounds like your mother's story is complicated, if it spans 60 years. Was that Uncle you mentioned, her brother?

"And to address your idea that you may be carrying something other than a spirit is completely right. We carry trauma in much the same way, and my simple methods work for both. When a person abuses you, or if you witness a violent act, the trauma can stick in you, and it can affect you continuously until you can find a way to begin to dissolve it.

"From a psychic perspective, both trauma and attached spirits look like densities in the human energy field. After several years of clearing people, my psychic partner and I realized that using your intention to Claim Your Space™ and receiving energy healing clears your human energy field, and even lifelong symptoms can be reversed. And I'm talking about emotional, mental and behavioral symptoms as well as physical. If you still feel like a walking time bomb, maybe we can get to the root of it... if you want."

Date: Apr 10

"I am going to tell a story. Not a good story. Very likely not even a believable story, but it is true. You may have assumed at this point, that this has to do with the occult. What I tell you is only my story. There is so much more to it. My brothers and sister have their own stories to tell. My mother and father also have their stories. I know a lot about all of them, but it would become a book if I wrote about it all.

"My very first memory in life is hearing a baby crying. I must have been about three years old. I have remembered that all my life. I asked my older sister (10 years older) why the baby was crying. She seemed very frightened and that frightened me. She told me she didn't know. My father was out of town playing baseball, and I didn't, at that time, know where my mother was. My older brother (4 years older) and my younger brother (18 months younger) were with my sister and me. The last of that memory was that my sister pulled me close to her and buried my face against her. She was shaking. My older brother later told me the reason for it. This will not make much sense because all the details are not included. If you want the whole story, I will begin writing it and send it to you. I will tell you, to clarify, that house we lived in belonged to my uncle. He had gotten my dad a job in a factory, and got my dad into sport activities that would keep him out of the house for long periods of time.

"It was a big old house - drafty - and it scared me. It had a long narrow stairway and at the top there was a hallway. There were several rooms along the hallway and at the end another room that was kept locked. A room I dreamed about all my life until the memories came back.

"I wanted to tell you my beginning of all of this.

"Now I will tell you of my mother's death. My Uncle died in church at the pulpit. He had a heart attack. He led a double life, of course. Shortly after that, my Aunt moved to St. Louis, Missouri. A few years later my father died after surgery. His last words to me as he squeezed my hand were, "You were always the strong one. Take care of your mother."

"About six months later, my aunt "talked" my mother into moving to St. Louis with her. I lived in Kansas City at the time. None of us kids wanted her to go, but she did. Six months later, she called to tell us she had met a very nice man, and was going to get married. We were happy for her. My aunt had introduced them. To make a long story short, he wasn't that nice. They were married for five years. When we would go to visit, he would ignore my mom even to the point of turning off his hearing aids. He was very short with her. More than once we all tried to convince her to come home with us, but she wouldn't. In her time in St. Louis, my cousin showed up to visit my aunt quite a bit.

"One day I got a call from her husband telling me my mom was sick. I left within the hour and when I got to St. Louis she was almost coma like. She could barely talk and had not been eating. I took her to the doctor. They found nothing. Said it was probably the flu. I stayed to take care of her and the next day took her to the hospital. They found that her immune system was not working as it should and she was very anemic. My step dad's concern was that she hadn't brought her glaucoma drops for her eyes. They transfused her, and within a couple of hours she was perky and talking. I stayed the night with her and we talked all night. She talked about her and my dad and their younger days. She was released in a few days, and told me to go on home to my family. Two weeks later I got another call. She was sick again. This time one of my brothers and sister went with me. We put her back in the hospital and they ran all kinds of test. They never did figure out what was causing the problem. We all stayed with her, and within a day she was back to normal, and we were all laughing and talking. She was again released.

"Eight days later I got another call. I called my brother and my husband, and I left for St. Louis. When we got there, she was in bed barely able to move. When my step dad walked in the room, she told us to get him out of there. Earlier she had to go to the bathroom and had fallen and he had kicked her. It was very late and she told us to get some rest. We went to lay down for awhile and I heard him to tell her to shut her damn mouth. I jumped up and went into the room. She was not responding. I called 911 and again we took her to the hospital. We went to emergency. Her eyes were blood red. I sat and sang the song my dad had written for her and told her dad was waiting for her, and she smiled. I knew she was going. I walked out to tell my brother. Her husband was off having coffee. The doctor came out and told us she was gone. They ask if we wanted them to try and revive her and we said no. She had had a brain hemorrhage and would never regain consciousness.

"I must tell you this. My step dad's first wife was found dead on their farm. At that time my step dad was with law enforcement in Las Vegas. She was alone when she died. Apparent heart attack. I was so angry when my mother died. It just did not feel right. After the funeral when we were at the house, one of the sister-in-laws pulled me aside and all she said was, "Your mother should not have died." With all that was going on, I didn't put it together until later. What happened was by chance, or was it? I was visiting with my sister-in-law about two weeks later. She started talking about a doctor who had tried to murder his wife with fire ant poison. Something clicked. I had seen that in my step dad's shed out back.

"I went home and got on the internet. I spent hours following links for symptoms. I couldn't get there. I was very tired, and I just said, "God, if I am right, let me find what I need." The very next link was it. Every symptom my mother had was there. You would have to know how it works to understand. Given in small doses over a period of time it can destroy the immune system and the death is caused by cerebral hemorrhage. It can't be detected in the system after 12 hours. "There is much more to it, but it would take awhile to explain. I sat back feeling like I had found the answer. I heard my mom's voice as if she were in the room. She said, "Now you know, let it go. It will be taken care of." My step dad gave me her wedding ring set and invited me to come and visit. I never could.

"I have just thought of something interesting. He died about two years ago. That is when my problems started.

"That is the story. Make of it what you will. Thank you for letting me tell you.

Jeannie"

More realizations. Also confirmation of the negative emotions – suspicion of murder, major victim/tyrant stuff.

Date: Apr 10

"Dear Kelly,

"I hope you don't mind, but I want to say something. The people out here in the "normal world" could never understand what's going on with me. I have lived a rather normal life. Raised a great family and have wonderful grandchildren, but have always been sad. I have love for my fellow man and my God. He has watched over and protected me my whole life; given me challenges and trials, happiness and joy. He leads us where we need to go. What I am trying to say is I'm glad I got on your blog. There is more in life and death than the eye can see and most don't understand that. The silent battle within me is real and someone knew I needed help to fight it."

Date: Apr 14

"Dear Jeannie,

"As I read your message, I am reminded of the many times in the New Testament that Jesus deals with spirits (demons they are often called in the text). And if you read the non-Canonical texts, there are even more references.

"The situation of spirit interference, whether by attachment or intent, is a real and significant problem, in my experience. And the problem of trauma that is heaped onto us in childhood by experiencing or witnessing traumatic acts, sticks to us and affects the rest of our lives.

"I hope I can raise awareness to this fact. Untold numbers of people are suffering and they don't know why, and medicine isn't going to help."

"Do you want me to look at all the possibilities, or do you feel you've figured it out?

"First I should say I am so sorry. You had a murderous uncle and a murderous step-father. It's mind boggling. (patterning)

"If you don't mind my asking, where was your mother while the baby was crying? And was the baby related to you? Even though the spirit of your mom said to let it go, it doesn't mean *she* did. I believe murder victims stay in the earth plane hoping to resolve the problem. That would include the baby.
"And the culprit often stays behind for a number of reasons.
"Why would someone marry women and then poison them? He must have been extremely damaged. I hate to think why he might have felt the need to silence them. And the spirit of his first wife should be counted among those who possibly have not gone to the Light.

"You mentioned once before that someone had murdered a child. Is that the baby you mention? That in itself must be terribly haunting to you. You have multiple spirits who may not have gone to the Light, because they died by suspicious means.

"Are you experiencing any weird activities or health problems now? How about your siblings?

"I just got an email from a young woman who said she felt she was raped by an invisible force.

"What I'm trying to figure out is, are you still trying to resolve some of these terrible issues? Do you feel they are still affecting your life? It sounds like you've been working on it in many ways, so I don't want to presume that you have more work to do. But when the memories stick in your gut, it can be an indication that the trauma is still there. I think my exercises and meditations can help with this.

"What an incredible story. You must have found yourself asking why these things were part of your life.

"Let me know how I can help.

Kelly"

Date: Apr 14

"Dear Kelly,

"I don't know why certain things come into our lives; to shape us into who we are, I guess. The step-dad was introduced to my mother by my uncle's wife. I feel like it was all part of one. I would very much appreciate it if you looked into it. I don't have everything figured out. In telling you my story I am feeling a little bombarded. Maybe that makes sense to you. I feel that there is good and evil around me. It feels like a boiling pot. I have one friend who tells me I don't seem my normal self. This all seems a little detached, but I am telling you feelings. I am looking at myself and giving you how I am feeling right now. **My medical problems are still with me. Every test done shows no problems.** I know they are from within. I just need to get to them. Shortness of breath, swallowing problems, anxiety attacks and several other things. Kelly, **I hadn't had to go to a doctor for years, but in**

the last couple of years I feel like it's one thing after another.

"The baby belonged to my step cousin. No blood relation. I have always been sensitive to things around me and I also believe that all spirits don't move on. Because of my involvement with so much pain, maybe I am more open to the spirits that need help to move on. I don't know. I do feel that it's not just one.

"This is my theory about the marriage. Once you have been involved with the occult, they keep track of you. My mother knew and remembered it all. What a terrible secret she had to keep. My brothers have had "visits" throughout their lives. My sister had threats. I have had visits also. All from members. In doing studies on the occult I found it very diverse. Many believe it does not exist, but others know it does and the network is mind-boggling. People involved in the one with my uncle were lawyers, doctors, law enforcement, church officials, and the next door neighbors. There is a special network set up in the LDS church in SLC, Utah just for investigations into occult activities in the church. They would deny it, but my brother has a good friend that is involved in these investigations.

"I have been trying to learn what I can about all of this, but there comes a time when I have to back out of it all for awhile. I have a life to live, and I don't want to keep it in a hole of darkness. I let it go several years back. Of course what happened had an effect on me, but thus far, I have never been in a padded cell. :) Along with the evil, I had a lot of love around me too.

"Now my concern is sending these spirits where they belong. Let them and me be at peace. I have been doing the clearing exercise, and will try your other suggestions. There are those who want to protect me, and those who want forgiveness, but there is one bad dude who keeps getting in my face. :)   In doing the clearings, I see a face of an outraged spirit. Please don't think me crazy. I am a very visual person. Feelings bring me visuals. Again, I thank you for your concern and help. Just knowing I have an ally helps."

Jeannie"

She really began to connect her symptoms to the possible spirits who may have been attached to her. She said a very important thing, *"I am looking at myself and giving you how I am feeling right now."* It is really important to try to take stock of exactly what's happening with you physically, mentally and emotionally, and to try to notice how you have changed over time. She also decided she was ready to send them on to the Light. I decided it was time to give her specific directions.

Apr 15

"Jeannie,

"I really believe in going with your instincts. After all, who would know better than you? I think we should assume that you do have more than one spirit attached to you, and that your symptoms belong to one or more of those spirits. And this has nothing to do with good or evil, necessarily. Spirit attachment happens, period.

"Panic attacks are a classic symptom of multiple attachment. Another classic symptom is when your medical tests all come out negative.

"It's possible your mother is with you. If she is, she can see who else is in your space. She may think she is protecting you, and maybe she is. She may be afraid to leave you with that scary guy. It may be her symptoms you are experiencing.

"Early childhood trauma fractures the psyche and sticks in your energy field. That can be the beginning of the susceptibility of haunting. Then you had so many immediate family members die under traumatic and suspicious circumstances. Their tendency would be to stay for their own reasons. And you, because of your early trauma, and compassionate heart, would be a perfect host.

"I know it must sound overwhelming, but I believe you can sit down, in a meditative state, with the help of a very spiritual and trusted friend, and conduct out loud dialog with whoever you think is in your space. You can ask questions, of your mother or others, and wait quietly until you get a thought, or a feeling or just "know" the answer.

"Before you start, you need to call on the highest spiritual beings you can think of. I always ask Archangel Michael for help in these situations. He helps remove the ones who don't want to go. Do all of this praying and asking out loud. You ask them all to assist you in claiming your space, and in guiding any earthbound spirits to the light.

"I think you should plan to try to clear everyone in one session, but save your mother 'til last. You can talk to her and ask her to help identify and clear the other spirits in your space. Ask her to stay until the others are gone, and when the coast is clear, she needs to go too. You can thank her for helping you do this, and let her know she has done you a great service.

"If you suddenly get the idea that your Uncle is attached to you, or someone else you recognize, remember that intense emotion is what keeps them stuck. If you cannot forgive, you are actually holding onto them. Now is the time to let go.

"You are letting go of all emotion associated with all of these people - guilt, rage, remorse, abandonment - because that is the glue that is keeping them stuck to you. Even if you're not completely sure you mean it, offer out loud forgiveness to your uncle, and whoever else. In some cases, you may feel the need to apologize, like maybe to your mother. Apologies and Forgivenesses are the magic keys to get these spirits to leave you and go to the Light.

"Then you say the Claim Your Space™ exercise out loud. State your full name and say, "I claim my space as my own.

Any other person, spirit, entity or energy form does not have permission to be in my space and needs to go now."

"As you're doing it, pay attention to the sensations in your body, your emotions, everything. Spirits get fearful when they think they are going to get kicked out, and you can suddenly have a flare up of symptoms. But no matter what happens - neck ache, anger, panic, whatever - don't stop. Keep claiming your space out loud until it feels like its calm.

"I guarantee you will get rid of at least some. But really intend to release ALL.

"One important thing is to let go of the idea of fearing the power of the dark forces. They cannot and WILL not get you. You are in complete control of your space. And you have Heavenly helpers who will take care of any sneaky ones."

"You may not figure out who the outraged spirit is, but if it seems mad at you, apologize to it. It may be leftover from a past life, and you may have no recollection why that spirit is mad at you. But it doesn't matter. Just apologize and then Claim Your Space™ again."

"If you know anyone who does Reiki or energy work, it's really helpful to have them putting the Light energy into you as you're doing the clearing, because it helps to dislodge the spirits. It helps them let go and begin their journey. And it fills you up with healing energy so you don't "miss" the energy of the spirits. Receiving the healing energy while you're claiming your space reduces the chances of re-invasion."

"And since you called on Beings of Light, Guardian Angels, Healing Angels and Archangel Michael, you can rest assured that all the earthbound spirits will be guided to the Light. They are in capable hands after they leave you. They will be free, and so will you."

"I hope you decide to go for it. I feel like you're building up your personal power to do this thing, and that you will be successful."

Date: Apr 17

"Well I think we did it! I know I have seemed like one strange person over the course of our conversations. I haven't quite been myself. I identified and released my mother and sister, my step dad, Rebecca (a child I took care of and loved in a past life), and my uncle. They are gone now. My uncle was the hardest. I sent him love and forgiveness and told him what happened was his destiny - that God was a loving and just God and go to the light. It was all rather a strange ending, but then again my whole life has been strange. I had support on this side and on the other side. The peace feels so good. I resolved other issues in the process. I have learned much from your website and counsel, how to restore my energy and shield myself.

"I am an intuitive. I call myself a mirror. I sense people and then show them themselves and work through their concerns with them. Anyway I could not restore my energy or shield myself from unwanted feelings, so I left it behind. I was getting burned out. To make a long story short, I have done several readings in the last few days. What a difference some knowledge makes. I plan on learning much more. I am a bit battle worn, but already some of the symptoms are gone. Thank you, Kelly. You have a good heart. I feel that you may have thought you were dealing with someone off the left wing, but all was as told. When the dam breaks the water rushes very fast and goes in many directions. That's the way I felt.

"Sincere thanks,

"Jeannie"

Claiming Your Space

Claiming your space, or clearing your energy field, is not something everyone knows about. But I believe that should change. Claiming your space is a simple, yet important task that should be incorporated into your daily routine. Like brushing your teeth and washing your hands, claiming your space protects you from invisible forces that can make you sick or perhaps even cause your death.

Once you understand that a human being is not just a physical body, but a complex matrix of energy systems, it becomes obvious that claiming your space is as important as running virus protection on your computer. By the time a person doesn't feel well, or is experiencing physical, mental or emotional symptoms, it is clear that the energy, or subtle, bodies are burdened with some kind of density. When a person sustains a density of some kind, it slows down the vibrational frequency of the whole organism, making it more vulnerable to further attack, including illness and attracting more densities.

This chapter includes several exercises that will allow you to continue healing yourself as you feel the need. These exercises are wonderfully validating and relaxing, and easy to do. It may seem ironic that the remedy for all of the frightening symptoms I have illustrated is so simple. But it really is.

The keys are:
- your attention
- your intention
- your effort.

Show the Source of All That Is that you are paying attention to yourself. Explore your own existence. Look for patterning in your life. Use personal intention to begin the process of healing. Intend to connect to the Divine. Use your effort to do these simple exercises. With these things, you can free yourself from unwanted attachments, and familiarize yourself with the workings of your energy bodies. You will become more in control of your own life than ever before.

I have compiled a list of questions to help determine whether someone may be afflicted with attached spirits. One cannot make assumptions based on a few "yes" answers that spirit attachment is definitely a problem. What we are looking for is patterning. I have given examples in previous chapters of what catches my eye in the responses.

This questionnaire may cause consternation among some medical practitioners in the mental health field. Many of the symptoms listed here have already been categorized and named. It is not my intention that my Claim Your Space™ routine takes the place of necessary medical and pharmaceutical treatment. It is my hope however, that if someone does have many of these symptoms, one might try the Claim Your Space exercises before submitting to a surgical procedure or a lifelong pharmaceutical regimen.

After all, if you Claim Your Space™ and nothing was there to begin with, you haven't done any harm whatsoever. With exploratory surgery, looking for the answer to mysterious symptoms, you are placed under general anesthesia, which is always dangerous, and at the very least, you are left with a scar. Nerves are severed, tissue is damaged, and sometimes organs are removed. With psychotropic or psychoactive drugs, it is my understanding that if you take even one pill, your brain activity is changed forever. I'm not sure the psychiatrists even tell you that as they prescribe these meds after a 20-minute interview. And we haven't even begun to discuss the expense of surgery or a lifelong prescription.

The most debilitating aspect of all is believing you are stuck with a symptom or condition you will never overcome. Why not try claiming your space and see if it will go away? What have you got to lose?

Because of the nature of spirit attachment, symptoms can vary widely. Your symptoms will depend upon the symptoms the person had before he or she died and became attached to you. You have a physical constitution specific to you, and then take on a whole separate set of symptoms. In addition, there are the symptoms associated with being the host of a foreign energy – fatigue, foggy memory, confusion, etc. I have included questions covering a wide range of symptoms and family history in order to determine what the affliction may be.

In certain cases, a person may need the guidance of an experienced depossessor. Like people, certain spirits can be very stubborn and uncooperative. When a person has a drug or alcohol habit, the attached spirits are along for the "high." Those spirits can be very persistent, literally driving you to drink. They can influence your thoughts and attitudes in order to get their desires met. When you realize you are dealing with alcoholic or drug (or sex) addicted spirits, you need to make a commitment to stop using your drug of choice, until the spirit realizes you really mean it, and finally leaves. Usually alcoholic or drug addicted hosts are hosting multiple spirits. The more bizarre a person's behavior is, or the more paranoid or panic ridden the host is, the more spirits he or she probably has attached. Those spirits can doggedly cling to their beliefs, refusing to grasp the reality of the situation.

The more the spirit resists going to the Light, the more frightened the host can become, and the more the spirit's symptoms will manifest in the host. So the situation can appear to become worse in the midst of the clearing. People have told me they have become nauseous, developed a fever, had difficulty breathing, passed out, become panic-filled. In the midst of claiming their space, their bodies have become heavy, they felt temporarily paralyzed, etc. Sometimes it's just the process of the spirit finally realizing it is dead, but I also believe it's a sort of protective mechanism, because if the host is suddenly in pain or distress, he or she may be frightened into stopping the process. And the spirit is allowed to stay. Calling in Archangel Michael and Guardian Angels at this point can usually do the trick. But if you can't get past the illusion of symptoms at that crucial moment, seeking the help of an experienced depossessor is recommended.

After sitting through what seems like hundreds of sessions, I have concluded it is possible to state your intention on your own and Claim Your Space™ successfully in many cases. Tricky cases involve spirits who are attached for emotional reasons, like anger, betrayal, guilt or desire for revenge. They're not necessarily evil, but they may be trying to affect you negatively for their own reasons. In those cases, an apology or gesture of forgiveness is usually sufficient to get them to let go.

But in many cases, spirit attachment is caused by confusion. And once you speak to the spirit in question and explain its circumstances, very often it will apologetically leave. If you brought a spirit home from the hospital, for instance, that person is very likely not even sure he/she is dead. If you witnessed a sudden death and brought the victim home in your energy field, that person may not realize he/she is dead. If there was a death in the family, whether a newborn or an elder member, or anyone in between, it is possible that spirit may stay in the earth plane and attach to a loved one. If your friend or loved one committed suicide, that person may have two issues. One, he may not realize he actually succeeded, and two, he may need to be told that it's okay to go into the Light. Often, the clearing session is an opportunity to explain to the spirits what has happened, and to reassure them of their next appropriate step.

First, let's start with where you are. The main purpose of this diagnostic tool is to look for patterning. Over the course of my journey clearing spirits, I saw many patterns emerge. I saw fully named and documented, even life threatening, conditions vanish after a person was freed from an attached spirit. Another purpose of the questionnaire is to give the client an idea which symptoms are considered red flags. Many people find themselves having a multitude of unexplainable symptoms, yet go see different doctors, trying to get them taken care of one by one, rather than seeing them as part of a whole. Many folks have stated that everything seems to "fall into place" after they take the questionnaire and discuss the possibilities. They say it begins to "make sense."

It might be a good idea to photocopy the next few pages and take your time with this questionnaire. If there are questions you cannot readily answer, try asking for answers right before you go to bed. Ask for the answers to come to you in the morning. Put a notepad next to your bed, so you can write down what you get. Also, pay attention to your emotions, as they are always important clues to what is happening. Remember, the emotions may not be yours.

Spirit Attachment Questionnaire

Do you suffer from anxiety or panic?

Have you been diagnosed with a psychiatric or mood disorder?

Do your moods change quickly for no apparent reason?

Are you or have you ever been suicidal?

Do you know anyone who has committed suicide?

Do you REALLY, REALLY miss one of your deceased relatives or friends? If so, who?

Has a loved one died, and are you finding that you now have similar symptoms to the deceased?

Have you been told you have "inherited" a disease that someone else in your family has already died of?

Do you have a chronic physical illness that won't go away, or that Doctors cannot seem to cure?

Do you have insomnia?

Do people ever say that you did or said something, but you have no recollection of doing or saying it?

Has anyone ever said that you talk in your sleep?

Did you suddenly lose your attraction to your mate, or suddenly decide to change your sexual orientation?

Do you hear thoughts in your head that are not yours?

Do you see people or things that others cannot?

Do you ever feel that you are not alone?

Over time, have you developed addictions to food, alcohol, drugs or behaviors you didn't have before?

Have you had a dramatic change in attitude or beliefs?

Have you ever engaged in self-destructive behavior – cutting your skin or hair, picking at your skin or face, battering yourself or other things?

Can you think back to the time when your habits changed? What happened around that time? Did someone pass away? Did you drink to blackout? Witness a traumatic event?

Did you suffer physical, sexual or emotional child abuse?

Were you ever tortured physically, mentally or emotionally?

Have you ever been under general anesthesia? List dates and reasons for the surgery.

Have you ever lost a child, born or unborn?

Were you a twin, but the other baby didn't survive?

Have you ever toured or lived near or fought in a battlefield or place of extreme decimation of human life? (modern war, Gettysburg, Auchschwitz, Hiroshima, Pearl Harbor, etc?)

Do you live near or spend time in a graveyard for any reason?

Have you spent time in a hospital, prison, convalescent home, treatment center - for work, to visit, or other reasons?

Have you ever used drink or drugs to the point of blackout (walking and talking, but not remembering a period of time)?

Have you ever used drink or drugs to the point of unconsciousness? List dates the best you can.

Are your symptoms similar to those of a family member?

◆●◆●◆●◆●◆●◆●◆●◆

Just doing the questionnaire and taking inventory is empowering and begins the process of your focusing inward. It begins the *attention* portion of your process. The next step is to view the questionnaire and look for patterning. Often, a memory will come up while answering the questions. It helps to list dates, specific symptoms, feelings, duration of suffering, and any other observations you may have. If you get a feeling that a certain person may have stayed with you after their death, go ahead and follow the directions below. If you know you are suffering, but aren't sure of the cause, go ahead and do the clearing exercises anyway, and see if you feel better afterward.

What to do if you think you're being haunted

After years of helping people overcome all kinds of symptoms from paralysis to panic to suicidal depression to congestive heart failure to compulsive smoking/ drinking/ drugging/sexing, I can say with confidence that disembodied spirits or ghosts or entities can intermittently possess you and interfere with your health and wellbeing, often unintentionally, but nevertheless. If they were human once, they need to be sent to the Light. And you can do it. Even if it's Uncle Joe, the spirit has to go (to the Light).

It is important to remember that once you decide to Claim Your Space™, any spirits you have on board are likely to become fearful. They have their own abandonment issues, and fear of going to the Light may have been one of the reasons they attached to you in the first place. Once you decide to, begin the process as soon as possible, and don't let any sudden flare-ups, panic attacks or weird, frightening symptoms stop you. Whoever it is that has lived in your energy field all these years is afraid to die. It will act up and try to discourage you from continuing your healing. So I hope, no matter how bad the symptoms get, DO NOT SLOW DOWN YOUR HEALING PROCESS. You are at the crucial moment. You must press on. Try to be in your witness as you realize, the symptoms do not belong to you, they belong to an energy form that has been sharing your thoughts, feelings and body. And you are now going to Claim Your Space™ and regain what was rightfully yours, all along. And you are going to help this lost entity get where it needs to go.

It would be ideal to have a friend or loved one do this with you, if you feel you need support. If you feel you lose perspective (the spirit's thoughts and feelings take precedence over yours), having an objective party there to help you can be comforting and effective, especially in times when you feel temporarily caught up in symptoms. At the crucial moment, even though they feel real, the symptoms that flare up in your body are *illusion*. Another person can remind you.

Even if you think it's someone who isn't harming you, please consider the spirit may be influencing you so subtly, you don't realize it. This process is done compassionately, with both your and the spirit's best interests at heart. I have had clients tell me that after claiming their space their energy comes back in a rush.

Claim Your Space™

1. Claim Your Space exercise/grounding exercise

2. Hot bath with salt

3. Stop using drugs and alcohol until they go away

4. Learn to meditate and open your crown chakra

5. Shield

6. Recapitulation exercise

I have vacillated about which process to put first, the grounding exercise or the claiming. It is true that doing the grounding exercise before beginning any session puts you into a deep state and enables more thorough healing. It is also true that a person who is loaded with spirits might not be willing or able to sit for 8 minutes and do a grounding exercise. In extreme cases, it's best to go ahead and do the claiming first. You can always go back after you've cleared the way somewhat, and do the grounding followed by additional claiming. claiming your space can require several sessions anyway, so you can save the grounding exercise for the second and each successive session thereafter.

If your situation is particularly difficult for any reason, you can call on Archangel Michael, to summon additional spiritual back up. Patty saw him in session more than once, but I'll never forget her first description. We were faced for the first and only time with what appeared to be the Grim Reaper, pulling the life energy out of a client, through the top of her head. It was clearly an emergency, so Patty called on Archangel Michael. One minute, when facing the Reaper, she had been full of fear and dread. The next minute, as she beheld the Archangel with her eyes closed, I could see an expression of awe on her face. She said he was formidable, wielding a large gleaming sword and wearing dark gray armor. She said he too was frightening, in a reassuring sort of way. She felt confident that no lower energy life form could withstand the power of Archangel Michael, not even the Grim Reaper. He took the reaper away, and our client became instantly well.

Later, when a client presented us with the book by Gary Leon Hill in 2005, we learned that he already knew about what he called "Archangel Michael and his Mercy Band of Angels." And after that, I read Dr. Carl Wickland, and he used very similar terminology. When reason wouldn't budge an attached spirit, he would direct the spirit's attention to "the Others" who were standing by. Those others were apparently Archangel Michael and his entourage. They take care of the difficult or reluctant ones. Don't hesitate to call him if you feel you need him. It's important to call on him out loud.

1. **Claim Your Space™ exercise.**
Say all of this out loud

"I ask my guardian angels and healing angels to be present with me now as I intend for the most appropriate healing to take place. I call on Archangel Michael (or Jesus or Mary or any Light Beings that work for you) to assist me in clearing any foreign energies from my space. Please help clear any entities from me, guiding earthbound spirits to the Light, and removing any other energies that are not meant to be in my space."

"My name is *(State your full name)*. I claim my space as my own. Any other person, spirit, entity or energy form does NOT have permission to be in my space, and needs to go NOW. If any relatives were attached to me, I give you a heartfelt farewell, and ask you to understand that, even though you didn't realize it, your presence in my space has been causing my body to be ill. Please look for the Light. Someone you know will be there, waiting to guide you into the Light. I ask my guardian angels and healing angels to assist any spirits or entities who are hiding or unable to help themselves, and guide them out of my space and into the Light, or wherever is most appropriate. I give thanks knowing it is done."

You can make a tape and play it at night while you're going to sleep. You can talk directly to the ghost and tell it that at some point it died, and no longer has a body. You can tell it, it was meant to go to the Light when it died. You can tell it, there is perfect forgiveness in the light (often they feel guilty about something bad they did in life and believe they don't deserve to go.) You can tell it, it is harming you and it needs to go to the Light. Usually, they don't mean to harm you. You can be kind and firm, like with a little kid that's annoying you and doesn't know better. You can be aware of and compassionate to the fact that this person-without-a-body has probably been stuck for a while and WANTS something to change.

2. Hot Salt Bath

If you feel you need to add some power to the Claim Your Space exercise, run a hot bath, and put 1/2 cup of salt in the bath. In general, salt is very pure. It has a powerfully purifying effect. Some say that a mixture of ¼ cup sea salt and ¼ cup Epsom salt is particularly effective. *There is a warning on the Epsom salts box that says not to do a salt bath if you are diabetic.* I haven't tried it, but everyone is raving about the Himalayan salts now. I would think they would be good to use because they haven't been refined. After you've been soaking and while still in the water, say out loud the Claim Your Space exercise (see Step 1). It should work like a charm.

3. Stop using your favorite drug, alcohol or other substance

If you have experienced a dramatic personality change, or a dramatic change in the volume of your drug or alcohol use, you might consider that the ghost attached to you is attracted to something you are doing, like smoking cigarettes or pot, drinking a certain kind of alcoholic drink or taking certain drugs. All intoxication, by drugs and all alcoholic drinks, slows your vibrational frequency and makes you more susceptible to invasion. At one psychic institute they used to say, "When you check out, you leave the door open." What that means is, if you alter your consciousness by becoming intoxicated, you are leaving your aura unprotected and susceptible to invasion. So, stop using your favorite substances for 4 or 5 days while you do the space claiming. You should add an out loud statement to your claiming, if drug or alcohol abuse is your issue. Tell the spirits they are out of luck because you would rather die than use that substance again. They might wait and hide for a few days to see if you really mean it, but if you are persistent, they will eventually leave you. You may realize after the clearing, that the compulsion to use was never even yours. You may find you don't want to use drugs and alcohol anymore.

4. Meditation, Grounding and Opening your Crown Chakra

Included in this book is my grounding exercise. See next page. It takes eight minutes from start to finish. I learned it from my Reiki teacher, Joy Metcalfe, and Patty and I opened every psychic healing session with it for years. At first, you may find yourself feeling impatient, wanting to skip the grounding. You might not understand the value of grounding, be reluctant to focus inward for a variety of reasons, or you may think it doesn't take that long to bring the Light through your body and send cords to the center of the earth. But it's really important to relax into it, focusing inward on each chakra. So much of our conscious time is spent away from ourselves. And those who have experienced physical or sexual abuse find it uncomfortable to "be" in their bodies. They tend to busy themselves with activities, or numb themselves with substances. But while you are out of your body, some energy form could be in there, having a grand old time at your expense. So the first and most important step in claiming your space is to actually "be" in your own space. It's like if you go on vacation, and you come back to your empty house to find that someone has moved in, in your absence. You must be home, verifying that this is *your* place, and that others do not have the right to be here, in order to evict them and get your space back.

You need a meditation that teaches you how to run grounding cords from the base of your spine to the center of the earth, then bring the earth energy back up the cords, through the bottoms of your feet, ankles, knees, thighs, hips and back to the base of your spine. Bring the Earth energy up bit by bit, through the center of your body, through your 2nd, 3rd, 4th and 5th chakras, and into the center of your head (6th) and finally out the top of your head like a fountain.

Then open the Crown chakra at the top of your head and intend for Divine Light, or Universal Life Force Energy, to come in through the top of your head, filling you up with Light as it goes down the middle of your body, down your arms and legs, out the bottoms of your feet and down to the center of the earth. I have included the transcript of my grounding exercise here, in case it comes in handy in writing.

Sit up nice and straight and:

Imagine 4 cords beginning at the base of your spine, one running down each leg to the floor, and two running from the base of your spine straight to the floor.

Run all four cords through the floor, through the earth's crust, all the way to the center of the earth, and anchor them there like the four legs of a chair.

Bring the earth energy all the way back up the cords, up through the bottoms of your feet, up your legs to the base of your spine.

Allow grounding earth energy to fill the area at the base of your spine (the root chakra, where we store all our survival issues)

Bring the earth energy up to the second chakra, about two inches below your belly button and let it fill up. Sexual relationship issues are stored here.

Bring the earth energy up to your third chakra, which is your diaphragm area, about two inches above the belly button. Earthly concerns and worries are stored here. Let that area fill up with grounding earth energy.

Bring the earth energy up to your heart, 4th chakra, and let it fill up. The heart chakra is about unconditional or "higher" love (presumably higher love than second chakra or reproductive or lustful love)

Let the earth energy go down both arms and out the palms of your hands.

Bring the earth energy from the heart up to your 5th chakra, in the throat area, and let it fill up. This is the area of self-expression and judgment.

From your throat chakra, bring the earth energy up into the center of your head or 6th chakra. In the center of your head are three endocrine glands, the pineal, pituitary and the hypothalamus. It is referred to in eastern practices as the Cave of Brahman. When you bring the Light in there during the next part of this exercise, those glands will transport the Light throughout your body via the endocrine system and connective tissues. But let's finish with the earth energy.

From the center of your head, let the earth energy go out the top of your head like a fountain (crown chakra).

NOW:

Through that same spot in the top of your head, bring in Divine Light.

Bring it in to the center of your head and let it fill up with Light. Imagine those glands filling up with Light and bringing enlightenment to every cell in your body.

Let the Light and earth energies in your 6th chakra blend to the perfect mix that's right for you, and let it expand out to the edges of your skin.

Bring the Light down to your 5th chakra, in your throat area, and let it fill up with Light. Let it blend with the earth energy to the perfect mix that's right for you and let it expand out to the edges of your skin.

From your throat, bring the Light down to your heart and let it fill up with as much Light as it can hold. Let the Light go down both arms and out the palms of your hands. In the heart, let the Light and earth energies blend to the perfect mix that's right for you, and let it expand out to the edges of your skin.

From the heart, bring the Light down to the third chakra, where we store all our earthly concerns, and let it fill up. Let all your angsts and worries just dissolve in the Light. Let the Light and earth energies blend and expand out.

Bring the Light down into your second chakra and let it fill up with Light. Mix with earth energy and expand out.

Bring the Light down to the base of your spine and let it fill up with Light (root chakra). Let any survival issues dissolve in the Light. Let the Light and earth energies blend and expand out to the edges of your skin.

Let the Light go down both legs, out the bottoms of your feet, all the way down your cords to the center of the earth and spill out the bottom there.

YOU ARE NOW COMPLETELY GROUNDED

For the purposes outlined in this book, this exercise is a preparatory step for the Claim Your Space™ routine. When you are really in your body, calm and focused, the healing tends to be much more profound. You also notice more thoughts and emotions and sensations when you are grounded. All of those things are clues to help you clear yourself.

Once you are in this state, you can sit and let the Light download for a while. The Light contains all the information you will ever need. Here is where you will find absolute truth. You can focus on areas of pain, bringing Light there until the pain goes away. Send love to others, to the planet, to your enemies. You can intend to scan your body for "cords" that other people may have attached to you, and intend to remove those cords, so your space is your own and you are not being influenced by anyone. You can do all kinds of things when you have time. When you don't have time for a longer meditation, the grounding exercise will set you up for the day. You will feel more in rhythm with life, more peaceful, more expanded. In that place, it is easy to remember we are all connected to one another, supported by the Universe.

From this place, plugged into the Divine Force, our intentions for healing go into the Collective Consciousness of Humanity and begin to heal everyone. Every minute that you can spend communing with God or the Oneness, not only are you giving yourself the best possible healing, you are making a significant improvement of the condition of the world. It is without a doubt the fast track to attaining good health and world peace.

Once grounded, claiming your space is more profound. You will receive information from your higher self or guides, and the clearing will be more effective.

5. Shielding

Once you are grounded and have claimed your space, you can intend for the Light to expand from the inside out, getting brighter and brighter until, in your imagination, you are absolutely glowing. Lower energy life forms (including ghosts, entities, negative thought forms, and even parasites, viruses and bacteria) can't tolerate the light and move out of your space. You can do this every day. It only takes a few minutes. It's GREAT protection. While you are connected to the Light in this meditation, you are downloading all the latest information from the Universe, or Source of All That Is. You are getting all the absolute latest upgrades.

6. Recapitulation Exercise

The purpose of this exercise is to rid yourself of any residual energies that may be in your body following any physical or emotional trauma - an act of betrayal, a relationship break-up, a violation, an assault. Those who have experienced trauma carry around a traumatic imprint in their physical and emotional bodies. If left unresolved, disease and illness often manifest in areas of traumatic imprinting.

The invisible scars become present as physical scars, disabilities or debilitations. Density builds up, like scar tissue, in the human energy field, and that density interferes with the free flow of energy necessary for you to feel complete and fully functional. On the emotional level it can manifest as lack of trust, depression or negative beliefs.

It is possible to remove such imprinting with this simple breathing exercise. You can do the exercise for events ranging from severe cases of abuse to minor events that happen in the course of the day. If someone was rude to you or hurt your feelings, and you can feel yourself internalizing anger or running a mental tape, quickly do the recapitulation exercise to get rid of the energy before it settles in and does you any harm.

This exercise is good for people in co-dependent relationship who feel trapped, hurt or negatively affected by the decisions of another. If you disentangle your energies using this exercise, it will remove the emotional charge, and you will feel relief and freedom. And often, the problems will resolve themselves effortlessly.

Recapitulation is an exercise where you turn your head from side to side, inhaling and exhaling. You will do a round of ten complete breaths.

First, sit up straight and ground yourself.

When you are fully grounded, imagine the person you are energetically entangled with - in front of you, facing you.

Inhale, turning your head to the left. On the inhale turn, envision pulling any of your energy back from the person you've been projecting anger, rage or blame at, and bringing your own energy back to you. You are going to pull out any residual energy of yours that my still be in him, including desire for revenge, desire for apology, desire to control, etc.

With each in-breath, you will scan every cell of his physical, mental, emotional bodies and human energy field, pulling your own energy out and putting it in a ball above your own head. You will reclaim and purify your long lost energy, and bring it back into your body at the end of the exercise.

On the exhale, turn your head from the left all the way to the right. Intend that you are scanning your entire being for energy that this person may have left in you, or that you may not have been willing to let go of. As you do this, you expel any energy that the tyrant might have left in you, or that you are holding onto, and sending it back to him.

You are going to vacuum your body and human energy field on the exhale, depositing this person's energy into a ball above his head. It would not be impeccable to force it back into him. Rather, put it in the ball above his head so that he can choose to take it back or not, but the energy is fully removed from you.

Do this inhaling to the left and exhaling to the right, slowly, ten times. All the while, visualize separating your energies. After the tenth and final breath, you will completely detach from all of the energy you have deposited above the head of your abuser.

Then, imagine the wonderful cache of your own new-found energy, in a ball above your head, being purified with Divine Light until it is absolutely glowing. This is a gift to yourself, this energy that you have been missing for so long. When you are ready, bring your new, purified energy in through the crown chakra, at the top of your head, and let the energy come all the way through your light body, coming to rest in the places that need it the most. Give thanks knowing it is done.

ଔ

I hope this chapter becomes worn out from use. I hope you will incorporate these exercises into your daily life. I really want people to realize that external forces have sought to gain control over us by making us afraid to be in our own bodies. We have been convinced that we do not have the knowledge or abilities to heal ourselves. By believing this, we have allowed a select few to create a giant, phenomenally lucrative industry at our expense. It is time for all of that to be reversed. *We* are the ones who hold the key to the bulk of our healing experiences and ongoing well-being. *We* have the ability to keep ourselves well, most of the time. And on the rare occasion that medication or surgery is truly necessary, then we will go to the self-appointed medical experts. But we come to ourselves *first*.

We don't need intermediaries between us and the Source of All That Is. We don't need to confess our sins to a third party in order to gain forgiveness. We are already forgiven. Didn't Jesus tell us that? Everything we need is within our grasp. Nichiren Daishonin, a Buddhist monk in 13th century Japan, was persecuted for decades because he professed that everyone has equal access to enlightenment – women, poor people, the uneducated, not just the elite few. We are all connected to the Oneness. Whether Christian, Buddhist or Other, every spiritual philosophy I respect reassures us of this fact.

It goes without saying that there are myriad methods from which to choose to keep yourself healthy and in touch with your body and soul. Everything from yoga, proper rest, proper diet and daily moments of introspection can help us stay in touch with who we really are, and what we are capable of. Let's claim our connectedness, claim our right to be here, in these bodies, in this life. Let us Claim Our Space.

Keeping Your Life Condition Strong

This final chapter addresses two recommended methods of spiritual self care. They include Reiki and a particularly effective method of prayer. I am offering you these vehicles as methods by which to keep yourself on an even keel, because these are the things that worked for me. By receiving Reiki treatments, or becoming a practitioner and treating yourself, you bring high frequency healing vibration into your body. It dislodges densities of all kinds, and encourages all your bodily functions to return to their normal rate. The prayer guidelines are adapted from my Buddhist practice. I have modified the terms very slightly so that anyone can use the method. The underlying concept is to offer appreciation for your life, apology for whatever you may have done wrong, and determination to do better from now on.

Reiki

Patty and I offered private and group sessions, free healing clinics, and classes in vibrational healing. I was also a Reiki complementary therapy provider for a nonprofit agency that served a population of chronically ill people. My clients have had miraculous results, with only two Reiki treatments per month. I offer it here in hopes that you, the reader, will seek out a practitioner in your area, so you may experience a healing session like no other, and so you might consider getting your own attunements, making you better equipped to heal yourself and others. When one person gets the attunements to heal a loved one, the benefits to both parties are immeasurable.

When a person chooses to go to an energy healer, he is acknowledging the existence of a Divine Source to which everyone has access, and is indicating a desire to be well. Taking that first step is half the battle. For people who are really bogged down with symptoms, going to an energy healer is an important boost. It's like charging your car battery. After the initial charge, the system begins to charge itself. Sometimes we need a jump start. That's how Reiki can help.

My psychic partner observed how the Reiki energy affected our clients as I was applying it. Her impression was that it goes in and recalibrates your organs and other parts of your body so that they are encouraged to vibrate at their original healthy frequency. It's like a tuning fork that encourages everything to find its natural tone or rhythm. It dissolves the rigid patterning, then "feeds" the parts of you that have been deprived of a healthy flow of energy all these years. It literally gets you up and running again.

Here are some examples of my experiences as a Reiki practitioner.

- After 7 treatments, one fellow went from being on death's door, extremely weak and practically unable to walk, with unstable liver and thyroid, to being stronger and healthier than he had in 22 years. On that seventh visit, he was euphoric. He decided to share the results of his most recent blood tests with me. His liver enzymes had gone from over 1000 to the normal range. His thyroid stabilized. His cholesterol dropped 200 points. I had already noticed that he was no longer using his cane when he walked, he was coming to our sessions without needing a jacket, and his mindset had gone from withdrawn and paranoid to sociable and humorous. He was relaxed and open, and talking about going back to school. Not bad for a guy who thought he was surely going to die, right before we met. We continued with distance Reiki so he didn't have to come for hands-on treatments. He called after two years to report that his liver and kidneys had healed completely, and he felt it was the Reiki that did it.

- One lady came for chronic back pain and upper respiratory distress. We found she was still carrying grief for her deceased mother, deep in her heart chakra. The nature of her grief coupled with her symptoms caused me to suspect that her mother might be attached to her. We claimed her space as part of the treatment. After she left, called to say that she had been trying unsuccessfully to quit smoking before the treatment. She said after the treatment, not only did she not have a cigarette, she did not have one craving. In addition, her depression and upper respiratory symptoms had lifted.

- Another lady came in with such intense lower back pain she could hardly move. During the treatment, my intuition guided me to ask about her relationship. She was being abused and felt trapped. It had been going on for many years. At the same time, she was a care provider for the abuser's mother. I felt that because of her compassionate heart, and perhaps some early childhood conditioning, she was taking on all kinds of suffering in addition to her own. She had a martyr-like attitude, but it was so deeply ingrained she didn't recognize it. All she knew was, she was miserable. I applied Reiki, using the Hon Sha Ze Sho Nen symbol, in case her symptoms stemmed from past life experience.

She called a few hours after the treatment and asked, "Did I tell you I was diabetic?"

I answered, "No."

She announced that several times per day, she tests her blood sugar, and that after our treatment, the levels had dropped into the normal range for the first time in several months. We were both elated. I saw her a few months later at the grocery store with her significant other. They seemed to be getting along fine, her physical movement was fluid and pain free, and it looked like she had lost several pounds.

- One client suffered from Lyme Disease. After having been misdiagnosed with Multiple Sclerosis for more than a year, he suffered three strokes. He had severe joint aches, muscle spasms and foggy thinking. He also suffered from depression. I worked with him twice a month and watched him get better and better. Soon he was able to go back to work, climbing ladders and painting houses.

I have had nothing but miraculous results with every Reiki client. I think it's completely amazing.

In addition to all the wonderful physical, emotional and mental healing it does, I discovered during the course of my spirit clearing sessions, that the Reiki energy helps to dislodge the lower vibrations stuck in the body (spirits, bacteria, viruses, karmic and traumatic densities, etc) and fills the void in the body after the attached spirit has departed, or density has dissolved. In cases of people who had spirits attached to them for a long time, the Reiki was invaluable in that it prevented any feelings of loss or grief, and greatly reduced the chances of re-invasion. I've had many testimonials of people who actually felt energy "shifting" in their bodies during a treatment, especially when used in conjunction with the Claim Your Space exercise.

In fact, the suicidal homosexual client with AIDS and neuropathy I mentioned in a previous chapter, said it felt like "Christmas lights" were going on and off inside his 'bad' leg. He had suffered from severe neuropathy and had been trapped in his apartment for several months because he had to descend 70 steps to reach the street. Both feet and one of his legs were numb. But they hurt at the same time. It was actually my first experience with neuropathy. I realized later, that sensation of "Christmas lights" was probably indicative of his deceased partner's energy moving out of him, and his own sensation returning. The neuropathy, severe depression and alcoholism did not belong to my client, but to the partner whose spirit never went to the Light. Where's a gay man gonna go? They are constantly told they are "damned" and so probably a man who dies of AIDS doesn't expect to go to the Light. So maybe he decided to hang around the apartment with his partner. Unfortunately the partner took on all the deceased person's symptoms. If I facilitated this "stuck" spirit in going to the Light, thereby relieving symptoms of the surviving partner, I consider that a good day's work; well worth the $25.00 voucher with which I was paid.

It's amazing how Reiki works. It's hard to explain, so I am grateful that I have the letter below, highlighting a student's firsthand experience with self-Reiki.

This is rather personal and I'll probably squirm as I write this, but I had an experience the other night as I was doing self Reiki, and I think it is important to share. I'll need to divulge some private info, so please try to keep confidentiality for me.

I've been low on sexual energy for several years, and feeling depressed about the future of my marital bliss in that regard. We've spent thousands of nights in the same bed without touching each other. Rather than blame my husband this time, I decided to send Reiki to my second chakra area.

I was in bed, ready to go to sleep. I did the symbols and placed my hands on my tummy, under the belly button. As I did so, I also spoke to my Reiki Spirit Guide and stated my intention for more sexual energy. I expected to feel tingly and just get more energy after a few minutes. But what happened was I began to have mental pictures, memories of various times in my life when I had been hurt in a sexual way. There were many pictures, jumping from early adult to childhood. There were also memories of issues that caused me shame that were about a sexual intention or dialogue, not even an act. There were also pictures from movies I had seen, and I realized that I had been traumatized by witnessing violent sex acts on the screen. I also had memories of times when a family member had been hurt, and again I was a traumatized witness.

I realized these events were "up for review and release" and that they had to be dissolved and removed before my feelings of sexual energy and satisfaction could be restored. So I tried not to re-identify with the feelings of violation and anger. Rather, I said goodbye to the images.

The next morning, I had my back turned to my husband, as usual, but for some reason, he wanted to give me some attention. I didn't have to say a word, or even make any inviting gestures. It was obvious to me he could tell on some level that things had changed. It was a very comforting morning, and it gave me hope.

I truly believe that Reiki can heal anything, and I thank you for sharing this amazing skill with me.

Reiki Symbols and What They Mean

The Reiki symbols allow healing to happen on all levels - physical, mental, emotional, spiritual and karmic. I won't tell you about all the symbols and their uses, but I will highlight a few, to help you understand the depths of the Reiki energy. There's one symbol, Hon Sha Ze Sho Nen, that cuts through time and space and heals all things. One of its translations is "No Past, No Present, No future." It's the acknowledgement that everything is happening now; therefore everything can be healed now. Many Reiki practitioners have limited knowledge of how to use this symbol, and sometimes think it is only used for distance healing. But it's a powerful tool for dislodging built up densities in your energy bodies. Having practiced Buddhism all these years, I realized right away the incredible value of the Hon Sha Ze Sho Nen symbol, and I use it during every healing. I have learned from experience that the root cause of an existing malady may be buried deeply in our being, most likely caused by a past life trauma. I would be remiss not to use it. Using that symbol with every treatment allows for the most complete and thorough healing to take place.

Patterning is what we are all battling against. It's just that most people don't know it or see it that way. Everything that happens in our past lives and early childhood is part of a "set up" that puts patterning in place. Over time the patterning becomes rigid, and we find ourselves limited, emotionally, mentally, physically. We find ourselves ill. The beauty of Reiki and other kinds of energy healing is, it goes in and (with your intention) begins to dissolve the rigid structure of your patterning. If you go shopping for a Reiki Master, ask her what she knows about Hon Sha Ze Sho Nen, and how she uses it in healing. Even if you know more than she does, you can simply ask that she use the symbol during the healing.

Another traditionally used symbol focuses on mental and emotional clearing. That one is called Sei-Hei -Ki. The Reiki Master envisions the symbol and thinks about your full name as he or she applies Reiki to your head. I usually tell the client what I am doing as I am doing it. Often, people can prolong their sense of illness with the beliefs they generate every day. After using the Sei-Hei-Ki symbol and sending energy into the brain, I can feel people relax more fully into the healing experience. They breathe more deeply and tend to interact more in the healing process.

Reiki transcends time and space. It can help you heal your life. There's no need to fear going about healing yourself. Please make every effort to learn techniques and keep yourself well. As they said in my Ayurveda class, *Loka Samasta Sukhino Bhavantu.* Let Everyone Be Well.

Prayer Guidelines

This particular method of prayer brings about results so obviously, you will absolutely notice the difference in your life. While some may say that you cannot attain such magnificent results without also chanting Nam Myoho Renge Kyo every day, I feel that the intention and effort used to do the prayer in your own way will still yield results.

Of course, if you want to radically change your life and build a new foundation based on a deep connection with the Oneness, I must recommend you try chanting Nam Myoho Renge Kyo - which means Devotion to the Mystic Law of the Simultaneity of Cause and Effect. It is called a Mystic Law because it is too profound to be fully understood by the limited human mind. When you chant, it activates a connection, and suddenly your whole life seems to be in rhythm with the natural workings of the Universe. Chanting and practicing true Buddhism is truly taking your life into your own hands and steering it in the direction of your heart's desire. It is my hope that with the information provided in this book you will go forth as a bright and shining human being, full of Light. If you use these practices, people will come up to you and ask, "What are you doing? You seem so different, so much happier!"

It is said if you use this format twice a day, preferably at twelve hour intervals, during your prayer time, you can eliminate deep karma and begin to create good fortune for yourself and your family, seven generations back and seven generations ahead.

Let me define karma for you here. Karma is action in thought word and deed. The Buddhists believe there are ten consciousnesses. The first five "consciousnesses" are known to most of us as the five senses. The ninth consciousness is known as the karmic storehouse. Everything you think, say and do is recorded in the karmic storehouse. Actions of kindness and compassion generate benefits in your life while unkind and harmful actions generate consequences. Karma is fluid, it changes with every thought you have, every word you utter and every action you take. The effects of your actions are carried with you from lifetime to lifetime. When it doesn't seem fair that one person has abundance while another lives in poverty, a Buddhist would say each person created his own reality based on his past actions in thought, word and deed. Therefore, by using a tool such as the daily prayer of appreciation and apology, you start off in a position of generating good karma each day. Your intent to create good karma and cleanse your thoughts, coupled with the effort required to undertake the prayer equals positive results in your life. If you couple that with chanting Nam Myoho Renge Kyo, it is said you can eliminate built up karma each time you chant the phrase. At a reasonable pace, you can chant the phrase about 1,000 times in 15 minutes. Chanting while you do the Appreciation and Apology prayer yields powerful results.

Appreciation and Apology

There are five parts to the prayer - appreciation, self-realization, apology, determination and desire. The order of the prayer is important. In the Buddhist practice, we read the prayer while we are chanting out loud the phrase Nam Myoho Renge Kyo. But you can try it while in a moment of meditation or contemplation, and see how it feels.

Appreciation

-for having a spiritual practice

-for being able to change my karma

-for being alive at this time

-for all the people around me

-for everything being a teacher for me

(Please note, "all the people around you" include especially those people with whom you have conflict or disagreement.)

Self-Realization

- For every external cause, there is first an internal cause

- Every hurt, anger, frustration, irritation or painful situation that occurs to me is my responsibility.

- My karma caused that to happen, or caused them to behave that way.

- I will turn poison into medicine.

- Become aware of my own internal "magnets" that drew such an experience to me.

- I alone, am responsible for raising my life-condition.

<u>Apology</u>

-for slander in Thought, Word and Action

-May I NEVER want to slander anymore

-Prayer of altruism - pray or chant for the health and well being of the person(s) involved, and that they may deepen their faith. Ask, "What can I do to rectify the situation?"

<u>Determination</u>

-To work harder for World Peace

-To create value in the areas of family relations, school, job or activities.

<u>Desire</u>

Only after praying for all of the above, chant for what you desire to manifest or achieve in your life. It is recommended to make a specific list for the things you need in your life.

When you get what you pray for and realize you need to refine your request it can be a process of elimination. For instance, after my abusive marriage was over and I wanted someone new in my life, I prayed to be adored. I didn't realize it at the time, but it was the polar opposite of being neglected, which is what I had experienced in the marriage. Well, I manifested someone who adored me, alright. He wanted to be with me every minute, move in right away, in fact. He watched me while I slept, wanted to take endless photos of me, showered me with compliments like – I was the most beautiful woman he had ever known. But the down side was he was irrationally jealous. He inspected my outfit before I went out and if my clothing looked anything other than absolutely plain, he would interrogate me about my motives. Pretty soon, I was miserable and had to pry him off of me and out of my life.

Needless to say, I needed to go back to the drawing board and refine my prayer.

When I pray for something big, like a windfall, I say something like, "I want the extra cash in my life to come as a result of my being on my path. I don't want to have to pay it back. No one will be injured in the process of the manifestation of this new wealth. When I am wealthy, I will share generously (with my religious organization, or with the needy, or whatever feels right). I don't want to have to work constantly, so that I lose contact with my family. I want to have time to be with my family and my pets." You get the idea. Be specific about how you want the benefit to look.

You can pray for the opportunity to develop your education, manifest a specific job, travel, find an affordable place to live with all the amenities you need - laundry facilities, pool, community garden, wall to wall carpeting, pet friendly, safe neighborhood - whatever it is you want. Specific parameters are good. And it is important to keep in mind, at least from the Buddhist standpoint, that you are manifesting everything you need so you can eventually focus your efforts on helping to promote and create world peace. Once all of your needs are met, you can spend your extra life force helping the world around you. You can teach someone else an effective form of prayer; you can help in a weather-related emergency; you can show appreciation to your elders in the family or in life. There are always opportunities to serve. Serving your fellow man is an important part of your spiritual practice.

ೞ

I have come to view certain actions as spiritual strategies. Doing something a certain way produces certain results. I was taught this at the very first Buddhist meeting I attended. It's all about how we are generating karma with every thought word and deed. When my first husband and I were divorced, he abandoned us financially. I was forced to spend a short time on welfare. I was very angry, feeling as if he was still victimizing us, even though we no longer lived together. A

Buddhist member suggested, "Maybe your ex-husband would pay child support." Knowing what I knew about my ex-husband, I felt he would rather go into hiding for the rest of his life than give his son and ex-wife a penny. But the Buddhist member said, "Pray for his happiness, and see what happens."

It seemed like the most difficult thing anyone had ever asked me to do. How could I shift from constantly blaming him for our misfortune, to praying for his happiness? I didn't want him to be happy; he didn't deserve it! I wanted him to suffer as he had caused us to suffer. But I had asked for change and was tired of being stuck in my own mental mire, so I tried it. As I was on my knees, chanting for the happiness of a man I despised, I was forced to recognize all of my own thoughts, words and deeds were my responsibility, including the thoughts in my head at the current moment, as well as things that took place during the marriage. I put him on my list of things to chant about in my twice daily practice, and within a few months, he called me of his own free will and stated he wanted to contribute to his son's well being. He wanted to pay child support. Buddhists call that "actual proof" the practice works. I wanted more actual proof. I wanted a normal life. I found effective prayer.

These are just two items that have worked particularly well for me. You can choose from a myriad of non-invasive healing techniques including meditation, other forms of prayer, chiropractic, acupuncture, hypnotherapy, diet, etc. They're all good. Seek modalities that feel right to you. The important thing is for you to consciously be on your path, dismantling limiting patterning and allowing Spirit the room to come in and be present in your life.

ଔ

Claiming your space of foreign energies, attitudes, ideas and addictions leaves you free to get to know yourself, feel your own energy, and be free to create your life the way you want it, rather than being limited by conditioning that has been thrust upon you by others. What has up to now been mysterious may become manageable, as you realize your symptoms and limitations have their roots in your human energy field. You don't need to surrender control of yourself to religious or medical authorities, blindly seeking external solutions to your inner problems. You can learn how you are built, so to speak, and become the mechanic of your own life.

Whether you are dealing with layers of trauma built up in this lifetime from victim experiences or being a witness of violent acts, suffering symptoms from an unknown source, or battling past life karma, using the simple techniques presented in this book can enable you to get your life under control. There's no need to seek external solutions which are often expensive and have side effects, until you've absolutely exhausted your God given powers of intent, attention and effort. If you sincerely try to take stock of your physical, mental and emotional symptoms, Claim Your Space™, find and use a good spiritual practice and have periodic energy healing treatments, you'll be very surprised how much progress you can make in alleviating your own issues. If you are able to get to know yourself energetically and bring about even the slightest relief using the information provided in this book, I will be happy. Please, Claim Your Space: *break the spell and be well.*

Made in the USA